Data LLM

Hands-on Guide to Using Large Language Models for Data Queries, Analytics, and Decision-Making

Charles Sprinter

Copyright Page

Data LLMs: Hands-on Guide to Using Large Language Models for Data Queries, Analytics, and Decision-Making
Copyright © 2024 Charles Sprinter

Disclaimer
The information provided in this book is for educational and informational purposes only. While every effort has been made to ensure accuracy, the author and publisher assume no responsibility for errors or omissions or for any consequences arising from the use of the information contained herein. This book does not provide professional advice and should not be considered as a substitute for consultation with qualified professionals.

Trademarks
All trademarks, product names, and company names or logos cited herein are the property of their respective owners. Reference to any specific product, service, or entity does not constitute an endorsement or recommendation by the author or publisher.

Table of Contents

Introduction

---

1. Why This Book Matters

1.1 The Data-Driven World: Opportunities and Challenges

We live in a world where data is the lifeblood of decision-making. Organizations, governments, and individuals increasingly rely on data to make informed decisions, whether it's understanding customer behavior, predicting economic trends, or optimizing internal operations. In this context, the term **"data-driven world"** has become more than a buzzword—it's a reality that shapes industries and lives.

Opportunities in the Data-Driven World

1. **Improved Decision-Making**:
   - Data enables businesses to make evidence-based decisions, reducing guesswork and increasing efficiency.
   - Example: A retail chain can analyze customer purchase patterns to optimize inventory and boost sales.
2. **Innovation and Competitive Edge**:
   - Companies leveraging data effectively can innovate faster, creating new products and services tailored to customer needs.
   - Example: Streaming platforms like Netflix use data to recommend shows and improve user experience.
3. **Operational Efficiency**:
   - Data analysis can identify inefficiencies and suggest improvements in processes, leading to cost savings.
   - Example: Manufacturing firms use data analytics to minimize waste and enhance production quality.
4. **Personalization**:
   - Data allows businesses to offer personalized experiences, increasing customer satisfaction and loyalty.
   - Example: E-commerce websites recommend products based on browsing and purchase history.

Challenges in the Data-Driven World
1. **Data Overload**:
    - The sheer volume of data being generated can overwhelm organizations, making it difficult to extract meaningful insights.
2. **Data Quality Issues**:
    - Inaccurate or incomplete data can lead to poor decisions.
    - Example: A financial institution relying on outdated credit reports might misjudge a client's risk profile.
3. **Complexity of Tools and Skills**:
    - Traditional data analysis tools require expertise in coding, querying, and statistics, which can limit accessibility for non-technical users.
4. **Ethical and Privacy Concerns**:
    - Handling sensitive data responsibly is critical to maintaining trust and complying with regulations like GDPR and HIPAA.

1.2 The Role of Large Language Models (LLMs) in Transforming

Data Workflows
Large Language Models (LLMs) represent a groundbreaking shift in how data is accessed, analyzed, and leveraged. These AI models, powered by advanced machine learning techniques, have unlocked unprecedented capabilities in data workflows.

How LLMs Work
LLMs like GPT (Generative Pre-trained Transformer) are trained on vast datasets containing text from diverse sources. This enables them to:
- Understand natural language queries.
- Generate human-like responses.
- Perform complex tasks like summarization, translation, and data extraction.

Key Advantages of LLMs in Data Workflows

1. **Accessibility**:
   - o LLMs democratize data analysis by allowing users to query and interact with data using natural language.
   - o Example: Instead of writing SQL code, users can simply ask, "What were the sales in North America last quarter?"
2. **Efficiency**:
   - o They automate repetitive tasks like cleaning and transforming data, saving time for analysts.
   - o Example: Automatically categorizing customer feedback from surveys.
3. **Adaptability**:
   - o LLMs can handle structured, semi-structured, and unstructured data seamlessly.
   - o Example: Extracting insights from spreadsheets, JSON files, and emails in a single workflow.
4. **Enhanced Insights**:
   - o By analyzing large datasets quickly, LLMs can uncover trends and patterns that might be missed with traditional tools.
   - o Example: Detecting subtle correlations in sales data across multiple regions.

Limitations to Be Aware Of

While LLMs are powerful, they're not perfect:

- They may generate inaccurate or "hallucinated" responses.
- Handling large datasets requires careful optimization.
- Ethical considerations, such as bias and data privacy, remain critical.

1.3 Real-World Examples of LLM Impact in Data Analysis

Let's explore concrete examples of how LLMs are transforming data analysis across industries:

Retail

- **Challenge**: A large e-commerce company struggled to analyze customer feedback at scale.
- **Solution**: Using an LLM, they automatically categorized reviews into actionable themes (e.g., shipping issues, product quality).

- **Outcome**: Customer support teams resolved complaints 30% faster.

Healthcare
- **Challenge**: A hospital needed to summarize lengthy patient records for quick decision-making.
- **Solution**: An LLM extracted key insights from unstructured medical notes, highlighting critical symptoms and medications.
- **Outcome**: Doctors saved hours daily, improving patient care.

Finance
- **Challenge**: A financial services firm wanted to monitor global market trends in real time.
- **Solution**: By querying financial news articles and reports using an LLM, they identified emerging risks and opportunities.
- **Outcome**: Faster decision-making improved portfolio performance.

Education
- **Challenge**: An online learning platform wanted to personalize recommendations for millions of students.
- **Solution**: LLMs analyzed past behavior and provided tailored course suggestions for each user.
- **Outcome**: Student engagement increased by 20%.

The combination of the data-driven world's opportunities and challenges sets the stage for tools like LLMs to become indispensable. These models are not only enhancing efficiency and accessibility in data workflows but also paving the way for new innovations. By harnessing the power of LLMs, individuals and organizations can unlock data's full potential, driving smarter decisions and better outcomes.

This book will equip you with the knowledge and tools to leverage LLMs in your own data workflows, whether you're querying databases, analyzing trends, or making critical business decisions.

2 Who This Book Is For

This book, **"Data LLMs: Hands-on Guide to Using Large Language Models for Data Queries, Analytics, and Decision-Making,"** is written with a wide range of you in mind. It bridges the technical and non-technical worlds, providing actionable insights for professionals working with data, as well as decision-makers seeking to leverage data-driven strategies.

2.1 Data Professionals: Analysts, Engineers, and Scientists
Why Data Professionals Need This Book
In today's data-rich world, professionals such as data analysts, engineers, and scientists face increasing demands to deliver faster and deeper insights. This book is specifically tailored for:

- **Data Analysts**: Who need tools to simplify data queries, perform analysis, and generate reports efficiently.
- **Data Engineers**: Who design pipelines and need solutions to automate data cleaning, transformation, and integration.
- **Data Scientists**: Who require robust methods to explore and model data, leveraging advanced tools like LLMs.

Challenges Faced by Data Professionals
1. **Time Constraints**:
   - Writing SQL queries, cleaning datasets, and generating reports can be time-intensive.
   - Example: Writing a query to calculate monthly sales trends for multiple regions might take hours.
2. **Complex Data Sources**:
   - Professionals often work with varied data formats, such as structured (databases), semi-structured (JSON), and unstructured data (text documents).
   - Example: Parsing customer feedback from emails and combining it with transactional data.
3. **Steep Learning Curves**:
   - Many traditional tools require expertise in coding or specialized software, limiting access to non-experts.
   - Example: Building visualizations or dashboards requires mastery of tools like Python, R, or Tableau.

4. **Data Volume and Complexity**:
    - The growing size and complexity of datasets make traditional methods inefficient.

How This Book Helps Data Professionals

This book introduces the use of **Large Language Models (LLMs)** to address these challenges by:
- Allowing analysts to use natural language to query databases instead of SQL.
- Automating repetitive tasks like summarization, data cleaning, and visualization.
- Enhancing exploration of massive datasets through advanced AI capabilities.
- Empowering scientists to model data with less manual effort, using insights generated by LLMs.

Key Benefits for Data Professionals

Feature	Traditional Approach	Using LLMs
Querying Data	Requires writing SQL queries	Use natural language prompts (e.g., "Show me monthly sales trends")
Exploring Data	Manual analysis with Python or Excel	Automated insights from raw datasets
Visualization	Build charts manually with code	Auto-generate visualizations from simple descriptions
Reporting	Time-consuming manual reports	Generate executive-ready summaries in seconds

Example Use Case for Data Professionals
Scenario:
A **data analyst** is tasked with generating a report on sales performance across 10 regions for the last year.
Traditional Approach:
1. Write SQL queries to retrieve sales data.
2. Import the data into Excel or a Python-based tool.

3. Generate charts and write a summary manually.

Using LLMs:
1. Input a prompt: *"Summarize last year's sales performance by region, and create a bar chart."*
2. The LLM queries the database, analyzes trends, and generates the chart and summary automatically.

Outcome: Task completion time is reduced from hours to minutes.

2.2 Business Decision-Makers and AI Enthusiasts
Why Decision-Makers Need This Book
Business leaders and decision-makers rely heavily on data to guide their strategies. However, they often lack the technical expertise to work with traditional tools like SQL or Python. Similarly, AI enthusiasts seeking to explore new frontiers may feel overwhelmed by the complexity of integrating AI into real-world applications.

Challenges Faced by Decision-Makers

1. **Accessing Insights**:
   o Decision-makers often depend on data teams for reports, leading to delays.
   o Example: A CEO needs a quick update on quarterly sales but has to wait for a detailed report.
2. **Understanding Data**:
   o Raw data or technical summaries are difficult for non-technical professionals to interpret.
   o Example: Complex visualizations without context can lead to misinformed decisions.
3. **Implementing AI Solutions**:
   o AI enthusiasts and leaders often lack hands-on knowledge to integrate AI into their workflows effectively.

How This Book Helps Decision-Makers
This book equips decision-makers with:
- **Natural Language Tools**: Learn how to use LLMs to extract insights directly from data using conversational queries.
- **Automated Reporting**: Generate executive-ready summaries and visualizations with minimal effort.

- **Actionable Insights**: Understand trends and patterns without requiring technical interpretation.

Key Benefits for Decision-Makers

Challenge	Traditional Limitation	How This Book Helps
Accessing Insights	Dependency on technical teams	Learn to extract insights independently using LLMs
Understanding Data	Overwhelming technical summaries	Simple, plain-language explanations for insights
Time-Consuming Reports	Long delays in report generation	Generate real-time insights and summaries
Exploring AI Tools	Complexity of coding and integration	Step-by-step guidance for leveraging LLMs in business

Example Use Case for Decision-Makers
Scenario:
A **marketing manager** needs to analyze customer feedback from social media to plan the next campaign.
Traditional Approach:
1. Gather raw feedback from multiple platforms.
2. Manually categorize the feedback into themes.
3. Spend hours drafting a summary.
Using LLMs:
1. Input a prompt: *"Summarize customer sentiment from this dataset and provide top complaints."*
2. The LLM processes feedback, categorizes themes, and drafts the summary in minutes.
Outcome: The manager has actionable insights faster, leading to quicker campaign decisions.

This book caters to both technical and non-technical audiences by providing a hands-on approach to using LLMs. For **data professionals**, it streamlines workflows, reduces repetitive tasks, and unlocks new analytical possibilities. For **decision-makers and AI enthusiasts**, it makes data insights accessible and actionable, bridging the gap between raw data and strategic decision-making.

By the end of this book, you will not only understand the power of LLMs but also feel confident in applying them to solve real-world problems.

3. How to Use This Book

This book, **"Data LLMs: Hands-on Guide to Using Large Language Models for Data Queries, Analytics, and Decision-Making,"** is designed to provide you with the knowledge and practical tools to harness the power of Large Language Models (LLMs) effectively. To make the most of this guide, it's important to understand how the content is structured and how you can actively engage with the material.

3.1 Chapter Overview and Learning Objectives

Each chapter in this book is carefully crafted to ensure a logical progression from foundational concepts to advanced applications. The content is structured to build your knowledge step by step, so you can confidently apply LLMs to real-world data tasks.

Chapter Structure

1. **Introduction**:
   - Each chapter begins with an overview of the topic, outlining what you'll learn and why it matters.
   - Example: A chapter on querying data will explain how LLMs simplify database interactions by replacing complex SQL commands with natural language queries.

2. **Core Concepts**:
   - Detailed explanations of the topic, broken down into simple and digestible sections.
   - Technical terms are defined in plain language, ensuring accessibility even for beginners.

3. **Hands-On Examples**:
   - Practical examples are included to help you see concepts in action.
   - These examples are explained line-by-line to ensure clarity.
   - Example:

python

```python
# Sample query using an LLM for sales analysis
query = "What are the top 5 products by sales this
quarter?"
response = llm.process_query(query)
print(response)
```

Output:
mathematica

1. Product A: $50,000
2. Product B: $45,000
3. Product C: $42,000
4. Product D: $40,000
5. Product E: $38,000

4. **Exercises**:
   - Each chapter ends with practical exercises that reinforce the material and challenge you to apply what you've learned.
   - Example: Create a natural language query to identify underperforming regions in a sales dataset.
5. **Key Takeaways**:
   - A summary of the most important points from the chapter to help you quickly review what you've learned.

Learning Objectives
Each chapter includes clearly defined learning objectives to help you focus on the most critical aspects of the material. These objectives ensure that by the end of the chapter, you can:
- Understand core concepts and terminology.
- Apply new skills to solve real-world problems.
- Gain confidence in using LLMs for data workflows.

3.2 Hands-On Approach: Exercises, Case Studies, and Resources

This book emphasizes learning by doing. Rather than simply presenting theoretical knowledge, it integrates hands-on activities that let you practice and master the use of LLMs in data workflows.

Hands-On Exercises

- **Interactive Prompts**:
  - Prompts encourage you to explore LLM capabilities actively.
  - Example:
    - Input: *"Generate a SQL query to find the average order value by month for 2023."*
    - Output:

sql

```sql
SELECT MONTH(order_date) AS Month,
       AVG(order_value) AS AverageOrderValue
FROM orders
WHERE YEAR(order_date) = 2023
GROUP BY MONTH(order_date);
```

- **Error Handling Scenarios**:
  - Exercises also include common issues you might encounter and how to resolve them.
  - Example:
    - Problem: "What happens if your LLM query returns incomplete data?"
    - Solution: Implement validation checks to verify query accuracy.

Case Studies

Real-world case studies are included to demonstrate the practical application of LLMs across various industries. Each case study includes:

- **Background**: An overview of the problem.
- **Solution**: Step-by-step implementation using LLMs.
- **Outcome**: The benefits and results achieved.

Example Case Study

Scenario: Automating Customer Feedback Analysis in Retail

- **Background**: A retail company wants to identify top complaints in customer reviews.
- **Solution**:

python

```python
# Using an LLM to summarize customer complaints
feedback = load_customer_feedback()  # Load feedback
from a dataset
prompt = "Summarize the top customer complaints from
this feedback."
summary = llm.summarize(feedback, prompt)
print(summary)
```

Output:
markdown

Top complaints:
1. Delayed shipping times.
2. Poor packaging quality.
3. Limited stock availability.

- **Outcome**: Faster response to customer issues, leading to a 20% improvement in satisfaction ratings.

Supplementary Resources
To enhance your learning experience, the book provides:

- **Practice Problems**: Additional problems to test your skills, with solutions included.
- **Sample Datasets**: Downloadable datasets for hands-on practice.

3.3 Companion Resources: GitHub Repository and Online Community

This book comes with a robust set of companion resources to support your learning journey.

GitHub Repository

The GitHub repository serves as a central hub for all the code, datasets, and additional materials referenced in this book.

What You'll Find in the Repository:
1. **Code Examples**:
   - Fully commented Python scripts for each chapter.
   - Organized by chapter for easy navigation.
2. **Datasets**:

- o Realistic datasets for practice, including:
  - Sales and marketing data.
  - Customer feedback text files.
  - Financial transaction records.
3. **Templates**:
   - o Pre-built templates for common tasks like querying databases, generating visualizations, and creating reports.

How to Access the Repository:
1. Visit the GitHub link provided in the introduction.
2. Clone the repository using the following command:

bash

```
git clone https://github.com/username/DataLLMs-
Companion
```

3. Navigate to the chapter folders for specific examples:

bash

```
cd DataLLMs-Companion/Chapter3
```

Online Community

The book also connects you to a supportive online community where you can share insights, ask questions, and collaborate with others.

Benefits of Joining the Community:
1. **Interactive Discussions**:
   - o Participate in forums on topics like LLM troubleshooting, advanced use cases, and industry trends.
2. **Live Q&A Sessions**:
   - o Regularly scheduled sessions with the author and other experts to address reader queries.
3. **Crowdsourced Learning**:
   - o Share your projects and learn from others' experiences.

How to Join:
1. Access the community link provided in the book.
2. Create an account to participate in discussions and events.
3. Subscribe to updates for new content and resources.

By following this structured approach—chapter overviews, hands-on exercises, real-world case studies, and companion resources—you'll gain practical experience and a deep understanding of using LLMs in data workflows. The integration of a GitHub repository and an active online community ensures you'll have continued support as you apply these techniques to real-world challenges.

4. Unique Features of This Book

This book, stands out because it provides not just theoretical knowledge but also a wealth of practical tools and resources. These features are designed to ensure a comprehensive, hands-on learning experience, bridging the gap between understanding concepts and applying them effectively.

4.1 Downloadable Code and Templates
One of the most valuable aspects of this book is the availability of pre-written, downloadable code and templates. These resources save time and effort, allowing you to focus on mastering the concepts rather than starting from scratch.

What You Get
1. **Fully Commented Code**:
   - Each code snippet in the book is available for download, complete with explanatory comments.
   - Code is organized by chapters, making it easy to follow along.
2. **Reusable Templates**:
   - Templates are provided for common tasks like querying data, automating analyses, and generating visualizations.
   - These templates can be adapted to your specific needs.
3. **Error-Handled Examples**:
   - The downloadable code includes built-in error handling to demonstrate best practices.

Example: Query Automation Template
Scenario:
You want to automate the generation of SQL queries using an LLM.
Code Template:

python

```python
# Import necessary libraries
from llm_api import LLMQueryProcessor

# Initialize the LLM Query Processor
llm_processor =
LLMQueryProcessor(api_key="your_api_key")

# Define your natural language query
query = "Retrieve the total sales by region for Q1
2023."

# Generate SQL query using the LLM
try:
    sql_query = llm_processor.generate_sql(query)
    print("Generated SQL Query:")
    print(sql_query)
except Exception as e:
    print(f"Error generating query: {e}")
```

Output:
sql

```sql
Generated SQL Query:
SELECT region, SUM(sales) AS total_sales
FROM sales_data
WHERE quarter = 'Q1' AND year = 2023
GROUP BY region;
```

How to Access the Code
1. Visit the GitHub repository link provided in the introduction.
2. Navigate to the corresponding chapter folder (e.g., Chapter3/QueryAutomation).
3. Download or clone the repository using the following command:

bash

```bash
git clone https://github.com/username/DataLLMs-
Companion
```

4.2 Real-World Datasets for Practice

To ensure hands-on learning, this book includes access to realistic datasets that simulate challenges you might encounter in real-world projects.

What's Included

1. **Structured Data**:
   - o Example: Sales, inventory, and financial transaction records in CSV and SQL formats.
   - o Use Case: Practice querying, analyzing, and visualizing structured datasets.
2. **Semi-Structured Data**:
   - o Example: JSON files containing customer feedback or product reviews.
   - o Use Case: Learn to parse and analyze semi-structured data with LLMs.
3. **Unstructured Data**:
   - o Example: Raw text files with customer service emails or social media posts.
   - o Use Case: Summarize and extract insights from unstructured text.

Dataset Examples

Dataset	Description	Format
Sales Data	Monthly sales records across regions and products.	CSV, SQL
Customer Feedback	Reviews and feedback from e-commerce platforms.	JSON, TXT
Financial Transactions	Historical transactions with timestamps and amounts.	CSV

How to Use the Datasets

1. **Load the Data**:
   - o Use Python libraries like pandas to load and explore the datasets.
   - o Example:

python

```python
import pandas as pd

# Load sales dataset
sales_data = pd.read_csv("datasets/sales_data.csv")
print(sales_data.head())
```

2. **Apply LLMs for Analysis**:
   - o Use LLM-powered tools to extract insights from the data.
   - o Example: Summarize trends from the sales dataset.

python

```python
# Summarize trends using LLM
prompt = "Summarize the key sales trends in this data."
summary = llm.summarize(sales_data, prompt)
print(summary)
```

3. **Experiment with Real Scenarios**:
   - o Modify the datasets or add your data to replicate real-world challenges.

4.3 Interactive Online Support and Updates

To provide continued learning and support, this book includes access to interactive online resources. These resources ensure that your knowledge stays current and that you have a platform to connect with other learners.

Interactive Features

1. **Community Forum**:
   - o A dedicated forum for you to ask questions, share projects, and discuss topics covered in the book.
   - o Example: Post queries like *"How can I use LLMs to analyze time-series data?"* and get feedback from peers and experts.

2. **Live Q&A Sessions**:

- o Regularly scheduled virtual sessions with the author or guest experts.
- o Topics may include advanced techniques, industry applications, or troubleshooting tips.
3. **Crowdsourced Projects**:
   - o Collaborative projects where you can contribute to open-source solutions using LLMs.

Regular Updates
The field of LLMs is rapidly evolving, and this book ensures you stay updated:

1. **New Examples**:
   - o Updated code snippets and case studies to reflect the latest developments.
2. **Emerging Trends**:
   - o Articles and resources on advancements like multimodal LLMs and real-time data integration.
3. **Errata and Improvements**:
   - o Corrections or enhancements to book content based on reader feedback.

How to Access Online Support
1. **Join the Community**:
   - o Visit the provided link and register for free.
2. **Explore Resources**:
   - o Access supplementary articles, tools, and bonus materials.
3. **Participate in Events**:
   - o Sign up for webinars and workshops announced via email updates.

The unique features of this book—**downloadable code and templates, real-world datasets, and interactive online support**—make it a truly comprehensive guide for mastering LLMs in data workflows. These resources ensure that you're not only learning concepts but also applying them effectively to solve practical challenges. Whether you're an individual learner or part of a team, these tools will help you achieve success in using LLMs for data queries, analytics, and decision-making.

5. Key Takeaways

This book, **"Data LLMs: Hands-on Guide to Using Large Language Models for Data Queries, Analytics, and Decision-Making,"** is designed to empower you with the knowledge and skills to harness the transformative power of Large Language Models (LLMs) in their data workflows. The following section outlines the key takeaways from this book and how they can significantly enhance your efficiency, effectiveness, and innovation in data-related tasks.

5.1 What You'll Learn and How It Will Transform Your Work

By the end of this book, you will have gained a comprehensive understanding of LLMs and their applications in real-world data workflows. Here's what you'll learn and how it will make a difference in your work:

---

1. Simplify Data Querying with Natural Language
What You'll Learn:
- How to use LLMs to write SQL queries and retrieve data from structured and semi-structured databases.
- How to automate data retrieval tasks by converting natural language prompts into precise queries.

Transformation in Your Work:
- **Faster Access to Data**:
    - You no longer need to memorize SQL syntax. Instead, you can use plain language commands to interact with your databases.
    - Example:

python

```
query = "Show me the total sales by region for the last quarter."
generated_sql = llm.generate_sql(query)
print(generated_sql)
```

Output:
sql

```sql
SELECT region, SUM(sales) AS total_sales
FROM sales_data
WHERE quarter = 'Q4'
GROUP BY region;
```

- **Reduced Dependency**:
  - Non-technical team members can access critical data without relying on IT or data engineers.

---

2. Automate Repetitive Data Analysis Tasks
What You'll Learn:
- Techniques to automate descriptive and predictive analysis using LLMs.
- How to perform time-series forecasting, anomaly detection, and other advanced analytics with ease.

Transformation in Your Work:
- **Save Time**:
  - Automate routine data analysis tasks, freeing you to focus on strategic initiatives.
  - Example:

python

```python
data = load_sales_data()
prompt = "Find and summarize the sales anomalies for
the last 6 months."
anomalies = llm.find_anomalies(data, prompt)
print(anomalies)
```

Output:
yaml

```yaml
Detected anomalies:
1. March 2023: Sales dropped 20% due to supply chain issues.
2. May 2023: Unexpected 15% spike in sales from the North region.
```

- **Enhanced Insights**:

- LLMs help uncover patterns and correlations that traditional tools might miss, leading to more informed decision-making.

---

3. Create Interactive and Dynamic Visualizations
What You'll Learn:
- How to generate visualizations like bar charts, line graphs, and heatmaps using LLMs.
- How to build dashboards that automatically update with new insights.

Transformation in Your Work:
- **Easier Communication**:
    - Generate clear and compelling visuals directly from your data, making it easier to present insights to stakeholders.
    - Example:

python

```
prompt = "Create a bar chart showing monthly revenue
for 2023."
llm.create_chart(sales_data, prompt,
chart_type="bar")
```

- **Improved Efficiency**:
    - Eliminate the need for manual chart creation by automating the visualization process, saving time and effort.

---

4. Enhance Decision-Making
What You'll Learn:
- How to use LLMs to simulate scenarios, perform what-if analysis, and provide actionable recommendations.
- Techniques to translate raw data into insights that drive strategic decisions.

Transformation in Your Work:
- **Better Decisions**:
    - Empower your team to make data-backed decisions with clear and concise recommendations from LLMs.

o Example:

python

```
prompt = "What would happen if we increase marketing
spend by 15% in Q3?"
scenario = llm.run_simulation(data, prompt)
print(scenario)
```

Output:
csharp

If marketing spend increases by 15% in Q3, expected sales growth is 12%, with an ROI of 8%.

- **Quicker Responses**:
  - o Make decisions in real time by leveraging LLMs to provide instant insights.

---

5. Streamline Reporting and Documentation
What You'll Learn:
- How to generate automated summaries and professional-quality reports using LLMs.
- Techniques to create reusable templates for reporting.

Transformation in Your Work:
- **Automated Reporting**:
  - o Produce executive-ready summaries without manual effort.
  - o Example:

python

```
prompt = "Summarize the quarterly sales performance
for the leadership team."
report = llm.generate_summary(data, prompt)
print(report)
```

Output:
mathematica

Q2 Sales Summary:
- Total Sales: $1.5M (up 10% from Q1)
- Top Region: West (35% of total sales)
- Key Trend: Increased demand for Product A in the North region.

- **Improved Accuracy**:
    - LLMs ensure consistency in reporting, reducing errors.

6. Integrate LLMs into Your Workflow
What You'll Learn:
- How to connect LLMs with existing tools and platforms like SQL databases, Python scripts, and visualization libraries.
- Best practices for scaling LLM-powered solutions in an enterprise environment.

Transformation in Your Work:
- **Streamlined Workflows**:
    - Reduce complexity by integrating LLMs into your existing data pipelines.
- **Future-Proof Skills**:
    - Gain expertise in a cutting-edge technology that's becoming a standard in the industry.

Summary of Key Takeaways

Area	What You'll Learn	How It Transforms Your Work
Data Querying	Use natural language for SQL generation.	Faster and more accessible data retrieval.
Data Analysis	Automate EDA, anomaly detection, and forecasting.	Save time and uncover deeper insights.
Visualization	Generate charts and dashboards with natural language.	Easier communication and improved stakeholder buy-in.
Decision-Making	Perform simulations and scenario analysis.	Make informed, real-time decisions.
Reporting	Create automated summaries and professional reports.	Reduce manual effort and improve accuracy.
Integration	Seamlessly connect LLMs with existing tools.	Streamline workflows and enhance productivity.

How This Transforms Your Career
1. **Efficiency Gains**:
   - Save hours of manual effort every week by automating routine tasks.
2. **Enhanced Skills**:
   - Become proficient in cutting-edge AI tools, boosting your value in the job market.
3. **Better Decision-Making**:
   - Drive strategic initiatives with data-backed insights.
4. **Professional Growth**:
   - Position yourself as a forward-thinking professional leveraging the latest technology.

By mastering the content in this book, you'll not only improve your day-to-day productivity but also gain the confidence and skills to solve complex problems, innovate, and lead in a data-driven world.

Chapter 1: Understanding Large Language Models (LLMs)

1.1 Introduction to LLMs

Large Language Models (LLMs) are a revolutionary class of artificial intelligence models that excel at understanding and generating human-like text. They have transformed how machines process natural language, enabling applications in querying data, automating tasks, and making decisions.

1.1.1 What Are Large Language Models?

Definition: Large Language Models are advanced AI models trained on vast amounts of text data to perform a wide range of natural language processing (NLP) tasks. They are called "large" because of their size—measured in the number of parameters (weights)—which enables them to capture complex patterns in language.

Core Capabilities of LLMs

1. **Natural Language Understanding (NLU)**:
   - Recognize and interpret user input written in everyday language.
   - Example:
     - Input: *"What is the total sales revenue for Q1?"*
     - Output: The model generates a SQL query to fetch the relevant data.

2. **Natural Language Generation (NLG)**:
   - Produce human-like text, including summaries, answers, or detailed explanations.
   - Example:
     - Input: *"Summarize the following report."*
     - Output: A concise summary of the key points in the report.

3. **Context Awareness**:
   - Maintain coherence over multiple interactions or across large text inputs.
   - Example: Analyzing a full document to extract key themes.

Key Features of LLMs

Feature	Description
Multilingual Support	Understands and generates text in multiple languages.
Few-Shot Learning	Learns new tasks with minimal examples.
Wide Applicability	Can be used for queries, summarization, translation, and more.

Why LLMs Are Revolutionary

Traditional NLP tools were limited to predefined rules or specific tasks, requiring manual updates to handle new contexts. LLMs eliminate these constraints by learning from massive datasets, allowing them to generalize across tasks and domains.

1.1.2 Evolution: From NLP Basics to Transformer-Based Models

The development of LLMs represents a significant leap in AI and NLP. To understand their power, it's helpful to review how NLP evolved over time.

The Early Days of NLP

1. **Rule-Based Systems**:
   - Relied on manually crafted rules for language processing.
   - Limitations:
     - Could not handle variability in human language.
     - Required frequent updates for new tasks.
2. **Statistical NLP**:
   - Introduced probabilistic methods to model language.
   - Examples: Hidden Markov Models (HMMs) and Conditional Random Fields (CRFs).
   - Limitations:
     - Required labeled data for training.
     - Poor generalization to unseen data.

The Neural Revolution

1. **Word Embeddings (2013–2017)**:
   - Models like Word2Vec and GloVe represented words as vectors in high-dimensional space.
   - Strength:
     - Captured semantic relationships (e.g., *"king – man + woman = queen"*).

- o Limitation:
  - Context-independent: The same word had the same vector regardless of its meaning in context.
2. **Recurrent Neural Networks (RNNs)**:
   - o Used for sequence-based tasks like machine translation.
   - o Strength:
     - Processed data sequentially, retaining memory of previous words.
   - o Limitation:
     - Struggled with long-term dependencies due to vanishing gradients.

The Transformer Era

The introduction of the Transformer model in 2017 revolutionized NLP. It addressed the limitations of RNNs by processing sequences in parallel while capturing relationships between all words using **attention mechanisms**.

Transformers vs. Earlier Models

Feature	RNNs/LSTMs	Transformers
Parallel Processing	No	Yes
Long-Term Dependencies	Poor	Excellent
Scalability	Limited	Highly scalable for large datasets

Transformers Paved the Way for LLMs: By enabling models to scale to billions of parameters, transformers became the foundation for state-of-the-art LLMs like GPT (Generative Pre-trained Transformer), BERT (Bidirectional Encoder Representations from Transformers), and T5 (Text-to-Text Transfer Transformer).

1.1.3 Key Models: GPT, BERT, T5, and Others

1. GPT (Generative Pre-trained Transformer)
- **Developer**: OpenAI
- **Purpose**: Language generation and general-purpose NLP tasks.
- **Key Features**:

- - - Pre-trained on vast datasets and fine-tuned for specific tasks.
    - Generates coherent and contextually relevant text.
- **Example Use Case**:
    - Input: *"Write an email to summarize Q1 performance."*
    - Output:

```vbnet
Subject: Q1 Performance Summary

Dear Team,

Q1 has been a successful quarter, with a 15% increase in revenue
compared to Q4.

Key highlights include...
```

2. BERT (Bidirectional Encoder Representations from Transformers)
- **Developer**: Google
- **Purpose**: Language understanding.
- **Key Features**:
    - Processes text bidirectionally (considers both left and right context).
    - Excels at tasks like question answering and sentiment analysis.
- **Example Use Case**:
    - Task: Classify customer reviews as positive or negative.
    - Input: *"The product quality exceeded expectations!"*
    - Output: *Positive*

3. T5 (Text-to-Text Transfer Transformer)
- **Developer**: Google
- **Purpose**: Treats all NLP tasks as text-to-text transformations.
- **Key Features**:
    - Converts inputs to outputs in a unified format.
    - Handles tasks like translation, summarization, and question answering.
- **Example Use Case**:
    - Task: Summarize a report.

- Input: *"The company reported a revenue of $10M, with an 8% increase year-over-year..."*
- Output: *"Revenue increased by 8% YoY to $10M."*

Other Notable Models

Model	Key Strengths	Example Use Case
XLNet	Handles permutations of text for better context	Improves document classification accuracy.
RoBERTa	Enhanced version of BERT with optimized training	Performs better in sentiment analysis tasks.
ALBERT	Lightweight, faster version of BERT	Ideal for real-time NLP applications.

LLMs like GPT, BERT, and T5 represent a significant leap in the field of NLP. By leveraging transformer-based architectures, these models have transformed how machines understand and generate language, making it easier than ever to perform complex data tasks. This chapter has laid the foundation for understanding the capabilities and evolution of LLMs, which you'll build on throughout the book

1.2 How LLMs Work

Large Language Models (LLMs) are powered by advanced architectures, training processes, and techniques that enable them to understand and generate natural language. This section explores their inner workings, including the **Transformer architecture**, the process of **training and fine-tuning**, and the concepts of **tokenization and embedding spaces**.

1.2.1 The Transformer Architecture Explained

The **Transformer** architecture, introduced in 2017, is the backbone of modern LLMs. Its revolutionary design allows models to process vast amounts of text data efficiently and capture contextual relationships between words.

Key Components of the Transformer

Transformers consist of an **encoder-decoder structure**, but many LLMs (like GPT) only use the decoder. Let's break down the architecture:

1. **Input Representation**:
   - Text data is broken down into smaller units (tokens), which are converted into numerical representations.
   - Example: The sentence *"Large Language Models"* becomes:

text

["Large", "Language", "Models"] -> [101, 102, 103]

2. **Self-Attention Mechanism**:
   - Self-attention allows the model to focus on the most relevant words in a sequence, regardless of their position.
   - Example:
     - In the sentence, *"The cat sat on the mat,"* the word *"cat"* influences the interpretation of *"sat"* more than *"mat"*.

3. **Multi-Head Attention**:
   - Multiple attention mechanisms work in parallel to capture different types of relationships (e.g., grammatical, semantic).
   - Example:
     - One attention head might focus on verb-object relationships, while another focuses on adjectives.

4. **Feedforward Neural Network**:
   - Each layer includes a feedforward network to process the output of the attention mechanism.
   - This helps refine the understanding of contextual relationships.

5. **Positional Encoding**:
   - Since Transformers process tokens in parallel (not sequentially), they use positional encoding to retain the order of words in the input.
   - Example:
     - The model distinguishes *"The cat sat on the mat"* from *"The mat sat on the cat."*

Advantages of the Transformer

Feature	Description
Parallel Processing	Processes multiple words at once, increasing efficiency.
Contextual Understanding	Captures long-range dependencies between words (e.g., across paragraphs).
Scalability	Can be trained with billions of parameters, enabling large-scale language understanding.

1.2.2 Training, Fine-Tuning, and Prompt Engineering
Training LLMs
Training an LLM involves two key steps:

1. **Pre-training**:
   - The model is trained on massive text datasets (e.g., books, websites, articles) to learn general language patterns.
   - Objective: Predict the next word in a sentence or fill in blanks (e.g., masked language modeling in BERT).

Example:
   - Input: *"The dog chased the ___."*
   - Output: *"cat"* (based on learned patterns).

2. **Fine-Tuning**:
   - The model is further trained on task-specific datasets to specialize in certain applications (e.g., medical summaries, customer service).
   - Example: Fine-tuning GPT on a dataset of legal documents to improve contract analysis.

Fine-Tuning vs. Pre-Training

Aspect	Pre-Training	Fine-Tuning
Purpose	Learn general language understanding.	Adapt to specific tasks or domains.
Dataset	Massive, diverse datasets.	Smaller, domain-specific datasets.
Computational Cost	High	Moderate

Prompt Engineering

Prompt engineering involves crafting input prompts to guide the LLM's output. The quality of the prompt significantly affects the model's performance.

Types of Prompts:

1. **Zero-Shot**:
   - o No examples are provided.
   - o Example:
     - Input: *"Summarize this article."*
     - Output: A brief summary of the article.

2. **Few-Shot**:
   - o Includes a few examples to guide the model.
   - o Example:
     - Input:

arduino

Example 1: Summarize the text: "Alice went to the market." -> "Alice visited a market."
Example 2: Summarize the text: "Bob attended a meeting." -> "Bob joined a meeting."
Summarize the text: "John wrote a book."

     - Output: *"John authored a book."*

3. **Chain-of-Thought**:
   - o Provides reasoning steps to guide the model toward complex outputs.
   - o Example:
     - Input: *"What is 12 * 4 + 5? Let's solve step by step."*
     - Output: *"12 * 4 = 48, and 48 + 5 = 53. The answer is 53."*

1.2.3 Tokenization and Embedding Spaces

Tokenization

Tokenization is the process of splitting text into smaller units (tokens) that the model can process.

Types of Tokens:
1. **Word Tokens**:
   - o Each word is treated as a token.
   - o Example:
     - Sentence: *"I love cats."*
     - Tokens: ["I", "love", "cats"]
2. **Subword Tokens**:
   - o Breaks words into smaller pieces to handle rare or unknown words.
   - o Example:
     - Word: *"unbelievable"*
     - Tokens: ["un", "believ", "able"]
3. **Character Tokens**:
   - o Treats each character as a token.
   - o Example:
     - Word: *"cat"*
     - Tokens: ["c", "a", "t"]

Embedding Spaces

Once text is tokenized, each token is converted into a vector in an embedding space—a high-dimensional representation that encodes semantic meaning.

How Embeddings Work:
- Similar words are placed closer together in the embedding space.
- Example:
  - o Words like *"king"* and *"queen"* are closer together, while *"dog"* and *"bicycle"* are farther apart.

Visualization of Embedding Space:

Imagine a 3D plot where:
- **"cat"** and **"dog"** are near each other because they're semantically similar.
- **"car"** and **"train"** are near each other because they're related to transportation.

Importance of Tokenization and Embeddings

1. **Efficient Processing**:
   - Breaking text into tokens allows LLMs to process language in manageable chunks.
2. **Semantic Understanding**:
   - Embeddings enable models to capture nuanced relationships between words.
3. **Flexibility**:
   - Subword tokenization handles rare words and typos effectively.

Example Workflow:

1. **Input**:
   - Sentence: *"Transformers revolutionized NLP."*
2. **Tokenization**:
   - Tokens: ["Transform", "##ers", "revolutionized", "NLP"]
3. **Embeddings**:
   - Tokens are mapped to vectors: [[0.5, 0.8, ...], [0.4, 0.7, ...], ...]
4. **Processing**:
   - The model processes embeddings through layers to generate an output.

Understanding the core mechanisms of LLMs—the Transformer architecture, training processes, and tokenization—provides a solid foundation for leveraging these models effectively. With this knowledge, you're ready to explore how LLMs can be applied to real-world tasks in data analysis and decision-making.

1.3 Strengths and Limitations

Large Language Models (LLMs) have emerged as transformative tools in artificial intelligence, enabling numerous applications across industries. However, like any technology, they come with strengths and limitations.

This section explores the **advantages** that make LLMs powerful and the **challenges** that users must navigate.

1.3.1 Advantages: Scalability, Versatility, and Accessibility
1. Scalability
LLMs are highly scalable, making them suitable for handling vast amounts of data and performing complex tasks efficiently.
How Scalability Works:
- **Massive Training Data**:
    - LLMs are pre-trained on diverse datasets that span billions of words and contexts, enabling them to generalize across tasks.
    - Example: GPT-4 has been trained on diverse content, including books, articles, and online text.
- **Parallel Processing**:
    - Transformers, the architecture behind LLMs, process multiple tokens simultaneously, which allows them to work efficiently on large datasets.

Applications of Scalability:
1. **Data Summarization**:
    - Generate concise summaries from long documents in seconds.
    - Example:

python

```
document = "This is a long research paper..."
summary = llm.summarize(document, max_length=200)
print(summary)
```

Output: *"This paper discusses advancements in renewable energy..."*
2. **Real-Time Analysis**:
    - Handle live data streams to extract insights.
    - Example: Monitoring social media for brand sentiment.

---

2. Versatility
LLMs can perform a wide variety of tasks without being explicitly programmed for them.
Key Capabilities:

1. **Language Understanding**:
   - Understands context and meaning across different languages and dialects.
2. **Task Adaptability**:
   - Perform tasks ranging from answering questions to generating creative content.
   - Example: Translate text, summarize articles, or even write poems.
3. **Domain-Agnostic**:
   - Can be fine-tuned for specific industries (e.g., healthcare, finance, education).
   - Example: A fine-tuned medical LLM can summarize patient notes or suggest diagnoses.

---

3. Accessibility

LLMs are increasingly accessible to businesses and individuals, democratizing advanced AI capabilities.

Accessible Features:
1. **Natural Language Interface**:
   - Allows users to interact with models using plain language.
   - Example:
     - Input: *"Create a bar chart showing monthly sales."*
     - Output: Chart generated using libraries like Matplotlib or Plotly.
2. **APIs and Open-Source Tools**:
   - Many LLMs are available through APIs (e.g., OpenAI API) or open-source platforms (e.g., Hugging Face).
   - Example:

python

```
import openai
response = openai.Completion.create(
    model="gpt-4",
    prompt="What is the capital of France?",
    max_tokens=10
)
print(response["choices"][0]["text"])
```

Output: *"The capital of France is Paris."*

3. **Integration with Existing Tools**:
   - o Easily integrate LLMs with applications like Slack, Excel, or custom dashboards.
   - o Example: Automate customer support workflows with an LLM-powered chatbot.

1.3.2 Common Challenges: Hallucinations, Bias, and Performance Costs

Despite their strengths, LLMs come with significant challenges that users must address to maximize their utility.

1. Hallucinations

Hallucinations occur when an LLM generates information that is factually incorrect or entirely fabricated.

Why It Happens:
- **Prediction-Based Learning**:
  - o LLMs generate text based on probabilities learned from training data. They do not "know" facts but predict likely outputs.
- **Lack of Domain Knowledge**:
  - o Without fine-tuning, an LLM may produce incorrect answers for specialized fields like medicine or law.

Example:
- Input: *"Who won the Nobel Prize in Physics in 2023?"*
- Output: *"Albert Einstein won the Nobel Prize in 2023,"* (incorrect, as Einstein's award was in 1921).

Mitigation Strategies:
1. **Verification**:
   - o Cross-check outputs against trusted data sources.
2. **Fine-Tuning**:
   - o Train the model on domain-specific datasets for improved accuracy.
3. **Prompt Engineering**:
   - o Design prompts that encourage the model to express uncertainty (e.g., *"If unsure, respond with 'I don't know.'"*).

2. Bias

Bias in LLMs arises when the training data contains imbalances or prejudices, which are then reflected in the model's outputs.

Why It Happens:
- LLMs are trained on large datasets from the internet, which may include biased or incomplete information.

Examples of Bias:
1. **Gender Bias:**
   - Input: *"A woman is..."*
   - Output: *"...taking care of children"* (stereotypical response).
2. **Cultural Bias:**
   - Underrepresentation of minority languages or perspectives.

Mitigation Strategies:
1. **Dataset Curation:**
   - Use balanced and diverse datasets during training.
2. **Bias Detection Tools:**
   - Analyze outputs to identify patterns of bias.
3. **Ethical Guidelines:**
   - Incorporate fairness and inclusivity into the development process.

---

3. Performance Costs

LLMs require substantial computational resources, leading to high costs and environmental impacts.

Challenges:
1. **Hardware Requirements:**
   - Training or fine-tuning LLMs demands powerful GPUs or TPUs.
   - Example: GPT-4 requires large-scale computing clusters.
2. **Energy Consumption:**
   - The carbon footprint of training an LLM is significant.
3. **Latency:**
   - Real-time applications may face delays due to processing requirements.

Mitigation Strategies:
1. **API Usage**:
    - Leverage hosted LLMs through APIs instead of training your own model.
2. **Optimization**:
    - Use smaller, more efficient models for simpler tasks.
3. **Green AI Practices**:
    - Adopt techniques like model pruning and quantization to reduce energy usage.

Comparison of Strengths and Challenges

Aspect	Strength	Challenge
Accuracy	Excellent for general language tasks.	Hallucinations for domain-specific tasks.
Adaptability	Easily fine-tuned for new domains.	Requires careful curation to avoid bias.
Scalability	Handles large datasets efficiently.	High computational costs.

LLMs are powerful tools with transformative capabilities, offering scalability, versatility, and accessibility. However, understanding their limitations—hallucinations, bias, and performance costs—is essential for using them responsibly. By leveraging mitigation strategies like fine-tuning, prompt engineering, and ethical guidelines, users can maximize the benefits of LLMs while minimizing their drawbacks. As you progress through this book, you'll learn how to navigate these challenges effectively to unlock the full potential of LLMs in your workflows.

1.4 Why LLMs for Data?

Large Language Models (LLMs) are reshaping how data is accessed, analyzed, and utilized. Unlike traditional tools, which often require specialized skills and labor-intensive processes, LLMs simplify and enhance data workflows with their natural language understanding and generation capabilities. This section explores the comparative advantages of LLMs over traditional tools and their unique benefits in data workflows.

1.4.1 Comparison with Traditional Data Analysis Tools

Traditional data analysis tools have been the backbone of data-driven decision-making for decades. However, they come with limitations that LLMs address effectively.

Traditional Data Analysis Tools

Traditional tools include software and frameworks such as SQL, Excel, Tableau, Python libraries (e.g., Pandas, NumPy), and statistical models. While powerful, these tools often require significant technical expertise and manual effort.

Strengths of Traditional Tools

1. **Specialized Functionality**:
   - Tools like SQL are excellent for structured database querying.
   - Python libraries are versatile for custom analysis and modeling.
2. **Efficiency in Defined Tasks**:
   - Tools like Tableau and Excel allow users to create complex visualizations and reports efficiently.

Limitations of Traditional Tools

Aspect	Limitation
Skill Requirement	Require knowledge of programming, querying, or tool-specific skills (e.g., SQL, Python).
Time-Intensive	Writing code, debugging, and refining analysis can take hours or days.
Rigid Workflows	Workflows are task-specific and may not adapt well to complex, multi-disciplinary problems.
Limited Accessibility	Non-technical users often rely on analysts or engineers to extract and interpret data.

How LLMs Compare

LLMs transform traditional workflows by providing an accessible and dynamic interface for interacting with data.

Feature	Traditional Tools	LLMs
Accessibility	Requires technical expertise.	Uses natural language, making data accessible to non-technical users.
Workflow Complexity	Requires manual coding and tool-switching.	Consolidates multiple workflows (querying, analysis, and reporting) into a single interface.
Adaptability	Task-specific; may need multiple tools for a project.	Versatile across structured, semi-structured, and unstructured data.
Speed	Time-intensive for custom analyses.	Instant responses to natural language prompts.

Example: Querying a Sales Database

1. **Traditional Approach**:
   - Write an SQL query:

sql

```sql
SELECT region, SUM(sales) AS total_sales
FROM sales_data
WHERE year = 2023
GROUP BY region;
```

   - Requires technical skills, familiarity with database schema, and debugging.

2. **Using LLMs**:
   - Natural language prompt:
     - *"Show me total sales by region for 2023."*
   - Output:

bash

```
Region    | Total Sales
-------------------------
North     | $500,000
South     | $450,000
East      | $300,000
```

West | $400,000

Result: LLMs eliminate the need for manual coding, significantly reducing time and effort.

1.4.2 Unique Advantages of LLMs in Data Workflows

LLMs are not merely alternatives to traditional tools—they offer unique capabilities that enhance data workflows in ways that were previously unattainable.

1. Accessibility and Democratization

LLMs make data workflows accessible to a broader audience, including non-technical users.

How It Works:

- Users interact with LLMs using natural language, removing the need to learn SQL, Python, or other technical skills.

Impact:

- **Increased Productivity**:
  - Teams spend less time translating business questions into technical queries.
- **Empowered Decision-Making**:
  - Decision-makers can directly interact with data without relying on analysts.

---

2. Versatility Across Data Types

LLMs handle structured, semi-structured, and unstructured data seamlessly.

Traditional Limitation:

- Separate tools are required for structured data (e.g., SQL), semi-structured data (e.g., JSON), and unstructured data (e.g., emails).

LLM Capability:

- Process and analyze all types of data using a single interface.

Example:

- Input:

- o *"Extract customer complaints from this dataset and summarize the top issues."*
- Output:

markdown

Top Complaints:
1. Shipping delays.
2. Product quality issues.
3. Poor customer service.

---

3. Automation of Repetitive Tasks
LLMs can automate tasks like data cleaning, summarization, and report generation.
Use Cases:
1. **Data Cleaning**:
    - o Identify and correct anomalies, missing values, or inconsistencies.
    - o Example:

python

```
prompt = "Clean this dataset and remove duplicates."
cleaned_data = llm.clean_data(raw_data)
```

2. **Summarization**:
    - o Automatically summarize lengthy reports or datasets.
    - o Example:

python

```
prompt = "Summarize this financial report."
summary = llm.summarize(report)
print(summary)
```

---

4. Enhanced Insight Generation
LLMs uncover patterns, trends, and relationships that traditional tools might miss.
How It Works:
- LLMs analyze data holistically, capturing nuanced correlations.
Example:
- Input:
    - o *"What are the emerging sales trends this year?"*

- Output:

markdown

Key Trends:
1. Increased demand for eco-friendly products.
2. Decline in sales of high-cost items in Q2.

---

5. Real-Time Interaction
LLMs respond instantly to user queries, enabling real-time decision-making.

Traditional Limitation:
- Querying and analyzing large datasets often take hours.

LLM Capability:
- LLMs provide instant results for even complex queries.

Example:
- Input:
  - *"Generate a real-time dashboard for monthly sales."*
- Output:
  - A live, interactive dashboard showing sales trends.

---

6. Multilingual Support
LLMs can work with multilingual data, opening opportunities for global applications.

Example:
- Input:
  - *"Translate this customer feedback from Spanish to English and summarize it."*
- Output:

java

Original Feedback (Spanish): "El producto llegó tarde y en mal estado."
Summary (English): "Customer reported late delivery and damaged product."

---

7. Cost and Resource Efficiency

By consolidating multiple tasks into one tool, LLMs reduce the need for additional software, training, or human resources.

Summary of Unique Advantages

Feature	Traditional Limitation	LLM Capability
Accessibility	Requires technical skills.	Understands natural language queries.
Versatility	Separate tools needed for structured and unstructured data.	Handles all data types in a single workflow.
Insight Generation	Manual analysis required for correlations.	Automatically identifies patterns and trends.
Automation	Data cleaning and reporting are time-intensive.	Automates repetitive tasks with minimal input.
Real-Time Interaction	Delays in query and analysis processes.	Provides instant results for real-time decision-making.

Large Language Models (LLMs) revolutionize data workflows by addressing the limitations of traditional tools and offering unmatched capabilities in accessibility, versatility, automation, and insight generation. Their ability to handle complex queries, analyze diverse data types, and automate routine tasks makes them indispensable in modern data-driven environments. As we explore their applications in subsequent chapters, you'll discover how LLMs can transform your data practices and unlock new possibilities.

1.5 Ethics and Responsibility

The use of Large Language Models (LLMs) brings immense potential for efficiency and innovation in data workflows, but it also raises critical ethical and legal considerations. These issues are especially relevant when dealing with sensitive or impactful applications, such as healthcare, finance, or public policy. This section explores two key areas of ethical responsibility: addressing bias in data analysis and ensuring privacy and compliance from the start.

1.5.1 Addressing Bias in Data Analysis

Bias in data analysis occurs when an LLM's outputs reflect unfair or unbalanced patterns present in its training data. This can lead to skewed insights or decisions that reinforce existing inequalities.

Understanding Bias

1. **What Is Bias?**
   - Bias refers to systematic errors in the model's predictions or outputs due to imbalanced or unrepresentative training data.
   - Example:
     - A model trained predominantly on Western-centric data might struggle to understand cultural nuances from non-Western contexts.

2. **How Does Bias Arise?**
   - **Training Data**:
     - If the training data contains biased or incomplete information, the model will inherit these flaws.
   - **Algorithmic Design**:
     - Models can amplify existing biases through the learning process, especially if the data is unbalanced.
   - **User Prompts**:
     - The phrasing or context of prompts can inadvertently trigger biased responses.

Types of Bias in LLMs

Type of Bias	Description	Example
Representation Bias	Training data underrepresents certain groups or perspectives.	A sentiment analysis tool trained on male-focused datasets might misclassify female-focused content.
Confirmation Bias	Model tends to favor or amplify patterns already prevalent in the data.	A news summarization tool prioritizes Western news outlets over global ones.

Type of Bias	Description	Example
Cultural Bias	Outputs reflect dominant cultural norms rather than diverse viewpoints.	Translating idioms incorrectly for non-Western languages due to lack of cultural understanding.

Mitigating Bias

Addressing bias is critical to ensuring fair and reliable outputs. Strategies include:

1. **Diverse and Representative Training Data**:
   - Curate datasets that include diverse perspectives, demographics, and languages.
   - Example:
     - Include global literature and non-Western media in training corpora to improve cultural understanding.
2. **Bias Detection Tools**:
   - Use tools to identify and measure bias in model outputs.
   - Example: Evaluate sentiment analysis models across different demographic groups.
3. **Human Oversight**:
   - Incorporate domain experts to review and validate critical outputs.
   - Example: In healthcare, ensure medical professionals verify model-generated diagnoses.
4. **Prompt Design**:
   - Craft prompts that explicitly guide the model toward neutral or balanced outputs.
   - Example:
     - Biased Prompt: *"Why are women bad at coding?"*
     - Neutral Prompt: *"What factors contribute to gender disparities in the tech industry?"*

Example Workflow: Identifying Bias

python

```
# Input a prompt for sentiment analysis
```

```
prompt = "Analyze customer reviews: 'The product is
expensive but high quality.'"

# Model output
response = llm.analyze_sentiment(prompt)

# Analyze bias
if "expensive" skews sentiment to negative
disproportionately, flag for bias.

# Adjust response generation
neutral_prompt = "Provide a balanced sentiment
analysis considering both cost and quality."
```

1.5.2 Ensuring Privacy and Compliance from the Start

Privacy concerns arise when LLMs process sensitive or personal information. Ensuring compliance with regulations and protecting data privacy are paramount to maintaining trust and ethical standards.

Understanding Privacy Risks

1. **Sensitive Data Exposure**:
   - LLMs may inadvertently expose private information during training or in their outputs.
   - Example:
     - A model trained on unfiltered emails might reveal confidential details in generated responses.
2. **Unintended Memorization**:
   - LLMs sometimes memorize specific data points from their training datasets, leading to potential leakage.
   - Example:
     - An LLM recalls a Social Security number that appeared in its training data.

Key Privacy and Compliance Regulations

Regulation	Region	Key Focus
GDPR	European Union	Protecting user data and ensuring

Regulation	Region	Key Focus
		consent.
CCPA	California, USA	Transparency and control over personal data.
HIPAA	USA (Healthcare)	Safeguarding medical records and data.
PDPA	Singapore	Protection of personal data in organizations.

Strategies for Privacy and Compliance
1. **Data Anonymization**:
   - Remove or obfuscate identifiable information from datasets before training.
   - Example:

python

```
import pandas as pd

# Anonymize dataset
data = pd.read_csv("customer_data.csv")
data["email"] = data["email"].apply(lambda x:
"hidden@example.com")
```

2. **Controlled Access**:
   - Restrict access to sensitive data during model training and use.
   - Example:
     - Use role-based access controls to ensure only authorized personnel handle sensitive data.
3. **Audit Trails**:
   - Maintain logs of data usage and model outputs to track compliance.
   - Example:
     - Record every instance where the LLM interacts with user data.
4. **Model Fine-Tuning**:

- o Avoid training on sensitive or proprietary datasets without explicit user consent.
- o Example:
  - ▪ Fine-tune LLMs with synthetic datasets that simulate real-world scenarios.

Real-World Example: Ensuring Privacy
Scenario:
An organization wants to use an LLM to analyze customer feedback emails.

Steps to Ensure Privacy:
1. **Pre-Processing**:
   - o Anonymize email content by removing names and contact information.
2. **Use Encrypted APIs**:
   - o Ensure communication between the LLM and the organization's database is encrypted.
3. **Compliance Monitoring**:
   - o Regularly audit outputs to verify no sensitive information is generated.

Code Example:
python

```python
# Anonymize input data
feedback = [
    {"name": "John Doe", "comment": "Great product!",
"email": "john@example.com"},
]
anonymized_feedback = [
    {"comment": fb["comment"]} for fb in feedback
]

# Input anonymized data to LLM
response = llm.analyze_feedback(anonymized_feedback)
print(response)
```

Balancing Ethics and Innovation

While addressing bias and ensuring privacy can be challenging, they are necessary steps to balance the ethical use of LLMs with their transformative potential. Organizations that prioritize these considerations build trust, reduce risks, and pave the way for responsible AI adoption.

LLMs are powerful tools, but their impact depends on how responsibly they are used. By addressing bias in data analysis, ensuring privacy, and adhering to compliance standards, users can harness the benefits of LLMs while minimizing ethical and legal risks. These practices are not optional—they are foundational to integrating LLMs into modern workflows.

1.6 Common Pitfalls and Troubleshooting

Large Language Models (LLMs) have the potential to revolutionize data workflows, but they are not without challenges. Common pitfalls such as misinterpreted prompts, inconsistent outputs, or errors in responses can hinder their effectiveness. This section addresses these challenges by highlighting the pitfalls users face and providing strategies to troubleshoot and improve the reliability of LLM outputs.

1.6.1 Misinterpreted Prompts and Model Errors
What Are Misinterpreted Prompts?

Misinterpreted prompts occur when the model fails to correctly understand the user's intent, resulting in irrelevant or incorrect outputs. This issue often arises from ambiguous language, lack of specificity, or limitations in the model's understanding.

Common Issues with Prompts
1. **Ambiguity**:
    - The prompt lacks clear instructions, causing the model to guess the intent.
    - Example:
        - Prompt: *"Explain sales trends."*

- Output: *"Sales have been increasing."* (insufficient detail).

2. **Overly Broad Prompts**:
   - The prompt is too general, leading to outputs that are vague or unrelated.
   - Example:
     - Prompt: *"Tell me about sales."*
     - Output: *"Sales involve transactions between buyers and sellers."*

3. **Complexity or Overloading**:
   - Including multiple tasks in a single prompt can confuse the model.
   - Example:
     - Prompt: *"Summarize sales, visualize trends, and suggest improvements."*
     - Output: Partial or inconsistent results.

4. **Incorrect Assumptions**:
   - The prompt assumes the model knows specific context that hasn't been provided.
   - Example:
     - Prompt: *"Find the top-performing regions."*
     - Model Error: *"I don't know what data to analyze."*

What Are Model Errors?

Model errors are inaccuracies or incorrect responses generated by the LLM. These can include factual inaccuracies, irrelevant details, or outputs that deviate from the intended format.

Examples of Model Errors

Error Type	Example
Factual Errors	Model fabricates information: *"The GDP of France is $10 trillion."* (incorrect).
Formatting Errors	Model output doesn't follow specified format: *"1. Answer 2. Answer"* instead of a table.
Logic Errors	Model fails to reason correctly: *"10% of $500 is $600."* (incorrect calculation).

Troubleshooting Misinterpreted Prompts and Model Errors

1. Refine the Prompt

A well-crafted prompt provides clarity and structure, improving the model's response.

Problem	Weak Prompt	Improved Prompt
Ambiguity	*"Explain sales trends."*	*"Summarize the sales performance for Q2 2023, focusing on regional trends."*
Broad Scope	*"Tell me about sales."*	*"Analyze the top 3 sales regions for Q2 2023 and provide key performance metrics."*
Overloading	*"Analyze and visualize sales data."*	*"Analyze sales data for Q2 2023. Create a bar chart showing sales by region."*

2. Use Step-by-Step Prompts

Break down complex tasks into smaller, sequential prompts.

- Example:
    1. Prompt 1: *"Analyze sales data for Q2 2023."*
    2. Prompt 2: *"Based on the analysis, suggest three key improvements."*

---

3. Provide Context

LLMs perform better when given specific context or background information.

- Example:
    - **Weak Prompt**: *"Summarize sales data."*
    - **Improved Prompt**:

bash

```
Summarize the sales performance for the following
dataset:
Region | Sales
North  | $500,000
South  | $450,000
East   | $300,000
West   | $400,000
```

4. Validate Outputs

Always review model responses for accuracy and relevance, especially for critical tasks. Tools like validation scripts can help detect errors.

Validation Example

python

```
# Example: Validate numerical output
response = llm.generate("Calculate the total revenue:
Sales = $500,000, $450,000, $300,000, $400,000.")
expected_value = 1650000  # Sum of sales
actual_value = int(response.strip().replace("$",
"").replace(",", ""))

if actual_value == expected_value:
    print("Output is correct.")
else:
    print(f"Output error: Expected {expected_value},
but got {actual_value}.")
```

1.6.2 Strategies to Improve Output Consistency
What Is Output Consistency?

Output consistency refers to the ability of an LLM to produce reliable and predictable results across similar tasks or prompts. Inconsistent outputs can lead to frustration and reduced confidence in the model.

Strategies for Improving Consistency

1. Use Structured Prompts

Structured prompts guide the model to produce outputs in a predefined format.

- Example:
  - Prompt: *"Summarize the sales data in this format: 1. Key Trends, 2. Top Regions, 3. Suggestions."*
  - Output:

yaml

1. Key Trends: Sales increased by 15% in Q2 2023.
2. Top Regions: North ($500,000), South ($450,000).
3. Suggestions: Expand operations in the East region.

---

2. Fine-Tune the Model

Fine-tuning an LLM on domain-specific data improves its accuracy and consistency for specialized tasks.

- Example:
  - Fine-tune an LLM on financial reports to enhance its performance in summarizing quarterly earnings.

---

3. Implement Few-Shot Learning

Provide a few examples in the prompt to guide the model's behavior.

- Example:

rust

Example 1: Summarize: "The product performed well in Q1." -> "Good Q1 performance."
Example 2: Summarize: "Sales dropped slightly in Q2." -> "Slight Q2 sales dip."
Summarize: "Revenue increased significantly in Q3."
  - Output: *"Significant Q3 revenue growth."*

---

4. Use Temperature Settings

Adjusting the temperature parameter controls the randomness of model outputs:

- **Low Temperature** (e.g., 0.2): Produces more deterministic and consistent outputs.
- **High Temperature** (e.g., 0.8): Generates creative and diverse responses.
- Example:

python

```
response = llm.generate(prompt="Summarize sales
data.", temperature=0.2)
```

---

5. Add Constraints

Specify boundaries or rules for the model's output.

- Example:
    - Prompt: *"Generate a one-sentence summary, no longer than 20 words."*
    - Output: *"Sales increased by 15% in Q2 2023, led by strong performance in the North region."*

Workflow: Combining Strategies

1. **Refine the Prompt**:
    - Specify task and expected format.
2. **Validate Results**:
    - Use scripts to check for accuracy and formatting.
3. **Iterate and Optimize**:
    - Adjust temperature, fine-tune prompts, or retrain on specific tasks if outputs remain inconsistent.

Summary of Pitfalls and Solutions

Challenge	Cause	Solution
Misinterpreted Prompts	Ambiguous or overly broad instructions.	Refine and structure prompts; use examples for clarity.
Factual Errors	Lack of domain-specific knowledge.	Validate outputs; fine-tune with domain-specific datasets.
Inconsistent Outputs	Model variability or randomness in responses.	Use structured prompts; adjust temperature for consistency.

While LLMs are powerful tools, effectively navigating common pitfalls like misinterpreted prompts and inconsistent outputs is essential for reliable performance. By refining prompts, validating outputs, and employing strategies like few-shot learning and temperature control, users can maximize the accuracy and consistency of LLMs in data workflows. These practices will ensure a smoother and more productive experience with these transformative technologies.

1.7 Key Takeaways

This chapter has introduced the foundational concepts and considerations necessary for understanding and working with Large Language Models (LLMs). By exploring their architecture, functionality, strengths, limitations, and ethical implications, we've laid the groundwork for leveraging LLMs effectively in data workflows. Below, we provide a detailed summary of the concepts and considerations covered.

1.7.1 Summary of LLM Concepts and Considerations
1. Overview of LLMs

LLMs are advanced artificial intelligence models trained on vast datasets to understand and generate human-like text. They serve as versatile tools capable of performing a wide range of tasks, from querying databases to generating creative content.

Key Capabilities
1. **Natural Language Understanding**:
   - Ability to comprehend and interpret user inputs in plain language.
2. **Natural Language Generation**:
   - Ability to produce coherent, contextually appropriate responses.
3. **Adaptability**:
   - Applicability to a variety of tasks and industries, including healthcare, finance, and education.

---

2. How LLMs Work
2.1 Transformer Architecture
- **Core Components**:
  - Multi-head attention for contextual understanding.
  - Feedforward layers for processing outputs.
  - Positional encoding to maintain word order.
- **Advantages**:
  - Scalability, parallel processing, and long-range dependency handling.
2.2 Training and Fine-Tuning

- **Pre-training**: General knowledge acquisition using diverse datasets.
- **Fine-tuning**: Task-specific adaptation for improved performance in specific domains.

2.3 Tokenization and Embeddings

- Text is broken into tokens and converted into high-dimensional embeddings.
- Embeddings allow models to capture semantic relationships between words.

---

3. Strengths of LLMs

LLMs offer significant advantages over traditional tools, transforming data workflows with:

1. **Scalability**:
   - Efficient handling of massive datasets and complex queries.
2. **Versatility**:
   - Seamlessly adapt to tasks like summarization, translation, and data analysis.
3. **Accessibility**:
   - Democratize data workflows by enabling non-technical users to query and analyze data using natural language.

Examples of LLM Strengths

Task	Traditional Approach	LLM Approach
Data Querying	Requires SQL expertise.	Plain language prompts (e.g., *"Show sales by region."*).
Report Summarization	Manual effort required for reading and condensing content.	Automated, context-aware summaries in seconds.

---

4. Limitations and Challenges

Despite their power, LLMs have notable limitations:

1. **Hallucinations**:
   - Models sometimes generate factually incorrect or fabricated information.
2. **Bias**:

o   Outputs may reflect biases present in training data.
3. **Performance Costs**:
    o   High computational requirements can make deployment resource-intensive.

Strategies for Mitigating Challenges
- Use prompt engineering to improve accuracy.
- Implement validation processes for critical outputs.
- Regularly audit models for bias and fairness.

5. Ethical Considerations
Ethical use of LLMs is paramount, particularly when handling sensitive data or making impactful decisions.

Addressing Bias:
- Curate diverse and representative training datasets.
- Regularly test models for equitable performance across different demographics.

Ensuring Privacy and Compliance:
- Adhere to data protection regulations (e.g., GDPR, CCPA).
- Anonymize datasets and use secure APIs to safeguard sensitive information.

6. Common Pitfalls and Troubleshooting
LLMs are powerful but prone to common pitfalls, such as misinterpreted prompts or inconsistent outputs.

Misinterpreted Prompts:
- **Problem**: Ambiguity or lack of clarity in prompts leads to irrelevant responses.
- **Solution**: Refine prompts to be specific and structured.

Inconsistent Outputs:
- **Problem**: Variability in model responses reduces reliability.

- **Solution**: Use structured prompts, adjust temperature settings, and validate outputs.

---

7. Unique Advantages for Data Workflows
LLMs excel in automating and enhancing various data tasks:
1. **Query Automation**:
    - Translate natural language prompts into SQL queries effortlessly.
    - Example:

python

```
prompt = "Get total sales for Q2 2023 by region."
query = llm.generate_sql(prompt)
print(query)
```
Output:
sql

```
SELECT region, SUM(sales) AS total_sales
FROM sales_data
WHERE quarter = 'Q2' AND year = 2023
GROUP BY region;
```
2. **Insight Generation**:
    - Summarize trends and patterns from large datasets.
    - Example:

python

```
prompt = "Summarize key trends in sales data."
insights = llm.generate_summary(sales_data)
print(insights)
```
Output:
markdown

Key Trends:
1. Sales increased by 12% in Q2.
2. North region outperformed others, contributing 40% of total sales.
3. **Visualization**:
    - Automate chart generation from data.
    - Example:

python

```python
prompt = "Create a bar chart for monthly revenue."
llm.create_chart(data, chart_type="bar")
```

8. Practical Applications
LLMs are applicable across industries, offering transformative potential:
1. **Retail**: Analyze customer feedback for actionable insights.
2. **Healthcare**: Summarize patient records and suggest treatments.
3. **Finance**: Automate portfolio analysis and fraud detection.

9. Looking Ahead
The capabilities of LLMs continue to evolve, with emerging trends like:
- **Multimodal LLMs**:
    - Models capable of processing text, images, and other data types.
- **Real-Time Applications**:
    - Using LLMs for real-time insights and decision-making.

This chapter has provided a comprehensive overview of LLMs, from their architecture and functionality to their ethical considerations and practical applications. Understanding these concepts equips you with the knowledge to navigate the opportunities and challenges of LLMs effectively. As you progress through this book, you'll dive deeper into real-world implementations and best practices for leveraging LLMs to enhance data workflows.

Chapter 2: Essential Tools and Frameworks

Large Language Models (LLMs) integrate seamlessly into Python-based workflows, providing a flexible and powerful environment for data querying, analytics, and decision-making. To maximize the potential of LLMs, it is essential to set up Python correctly and install the right libraries. This chapter provides step-by-step guidance on preparing your environment for data workflows powered by LLMs.

2.1 Getting Started

This section covers how to set up Python and configure the essential libraries you'll need for working with LLMs in data-centric tasks.

2.1.1 Setting Up Python for Data LLM Workflows

Python is the preferred programming language for working with LLMs due to its simplicity, extensive libraries, and compatibility with LLM APIs. Here's how to set up Python effectively for LLM-powered workflows.

1. Installing Python

Ensure you have Python 3.8 or higher installed, as most LLM libraries and frameworks require a modern Python version.

Steps to Install Python

1. **Download Python**:
   - o Visit the official Python website.
   - o Choose the version compatible with your operating system (Windows, macOS, or Linux).
2. **Install Python**:
   - o Run the installer and ensure you check the option *"Add Python to PATH"* during installation.
3. **Verify Installation**:
   - o Open a terminal or command prompt and type:

bash

```
python --version
```

Output Example:

Python 3.10.4

---

2. Setting Up a Virtual Environment
Using virtual environments helps isolate project dependencies, preventing conflicts between different Python packages.

Creating a Virtual Environment
   1. **Navigate to Your Project Directory**:
bash

```
cd path/to/your/project
```
   2. **Create a Virtual Environment**:
bash

```
python -m venv env
```
   3. **Activate the Virtual Environment**:
         o   On Windows:
bash

```
.\env\Scripts\activate
```
         o   On macOS/Linux:
bash

```
source env/bin/activate
```
   4. **Confirm Activation**:
         o   Your terminal prompt should show (env).
Deactivating the Virtual Environment
To exit the virtual environment, simply type:
bash

```
deactivate
```

---

3. Installing a Package Manager

Ensure that pip, Python's package manager, is up to date to install the libraries required for LLM workflows.

bash

```
python -m pip install --upgrade pip
```

Output Example:

Successfully installed pip-23.0.1

2.1.2 Installing and Configuring Essential Libraries

LLM workflows rely on specific libraries for API interaction, data processing, and visualization. Below is a detailed guide to installing and configuring these libraries.

---

1. Core Libraries for LLM Integration

Library	Purpose	Installation Command
OpenAI	Access OpenAI's LLMs like GPT.	pip install openai
Hugging Face	Work with open-source LLMs (e.g., GPT-2, BERT).	pip install transformers
LangChain	Build pipelines and workflows around LLMs.	pip install langchain

Configuration Example: OpenAI API
  1. **Install the OpenAI Library**:

bash

```
pip install openai
```

  2. **Set Up API Key**:
      ○ Obtain your API key from the OpenAI platform.
      ○ Add the API key to your environment variables for security.

bash

```
export OPENAI_API_KEY="your_api_key_here"
```

3. **Test the Installation**:

python

```
import openai

response = openai.Completion.create(
    model="text-davinci-003",
    prompt="Summarize the benefits of data-driven
decision-making.",
    max_tokens=50
)
print(response.choices[0].text.strip())
```

Output Example:

Data-driven decision-making improves accuracy, efficiency, and accountability, enabling better insights and strategic choices.

---

2. Libraries for Data Processing

Library	Purpose	Installation Command
Pandas	Data manipulation and analysis.	pip install pandas
NumPy	Numerical computations.	pip install numpy

Example: Data Preparation with Pandas

python

```
import pandas as pd

# Load a sample dataset
data = pd.DataFrame({
    "Region": ["North", "South", "East", "West"],
    "Sales": [500000, 450000, 300000, 400000]
})

# Display dataset
print(data)
```

Output:

mathematica

```
   Region  Sales
0  North   500000
1  South   450000
2  East    300000
3  West    400000
```

---

3. Libraries for Data Visualization

Library	Purpose	Installation Command
Matplotlib	Basic plotting and visualization.	pip install matplotlib
Plotly	Interactive visualizations.	pip install plotly

Example: Visualizing Sales Data

python

```python
import matplotlib.pyplot as plt

# Sample sales data
regions = ["North", "South", "East", "West"]
sales = [500000, 450000, 300000, 400000]

# Create a bar chart
plt.bar(regions, sales)
plt.title("Sales by Region")
plt.xlabel("Region")
plt.ylabel("Sales")
plt.show()
```

Output: A bar chart showing sales distribution by region.

---

4. Libraries for Workflow Management

Library	Purpose	Installation Command
SQLAlchemy	Query databases programmatically.	pip install sqlalchemy
Streamlit	Build data-driven web apps.	pip install streamlit

Verifying the Setup

Run the following script to verify that all essential libraries are installed and configured:
python

```python
import openai
import pandas as pd
import matplotlib.pyplot as plt

# Verify OpenAI
try:
    print("OpenAI library is installed.")
except ImportError:
    print("OpenAI library is missing.")

# Verify Pandas
try:
    pd.DataFrame({"Test": [1, 2, 3]})
    print("Pandas is working.")
except ImportError:
    print("Pandas library is missing.")

# Verify Matplotlib
try:
    plt.plot([1, 2, 3], [4, 5, 6])
    print("Matplotlib is working.")
except ImportError:
    print("Matplotlib library is missing.")
```

Output Example:
csharp

```
OpenAl library is installed.
Pandas is working.
Matplotlib is working.
```

Conclusion

This section has provided a detailed guide to setting up Python and essential libraries for LLM-based data workflows. By following these steps, you now have a robust environment ready to explore the full potential of LLMs. The next sections will delve into how to use these tools effectively for querying, analyzing, and visualizing data.

2.2 Key Tools and Libraries

To effectively utilize Large Language Models (LLMs) for data workflows, it's essential to leverage a combination of powerful tools and libraries. These tools facilitate everything from LLM integration and API interaction to data querying, analysis, and visualization. This section provides an exhaustive overview of these key tools and libraries, including their use cases and implementation.

2.2.1 Overview of LangChain, Hugging Face, OpenAI, and Pinecone
1. LangChain
LangChain is a framework designed to build applications around LLMs, making it easier to manage complex workflows.

Key Features
- **Prompt Management**:
  - Enables reusable and structured prompt templates.
- **Chain Building**:
  - Links multiple LLM calls into a cohesive pipeline (e.g., query, summarize, and analyze).
- **Tool Integration**:
  - Works seamlessly with APIs, databases, and other frameworks.

Installation

bash

```
pip install langchain
```
Example: Building a Query Chain
python

```
from langchain.chains import LLMChain
from langchain.prompts import PromptTemplate
from langchain.llms import OpenAI
```

```python
# Initialize the LLM
llm = OpenAI(model="text-davinci-003", temperature=0)

# Create a prompt template
prompt = PromptTemplate(
    input_variables=["region"],
    template="Summarize sales data trends for the
{region} region."
)

# Build a chain
chain = LLMChain(llm=llm, prompt=prompt)

# Run the chain
response = chain.run(region="North")
print(response)
```

2. Hugging Face
Hugging Face provides open-source models, tools, and datasets, making it ideal for experimentation and deployment of custom LLMs.

Key Features
- **Pre-Trained Models**:
    - Access to popular models like GPT-2, BERT, and T5.
- **Fine-Tuning**:
    - Customize models for specific tasks or industries.
- **Transformers Library**:
    - Core library for working with NLP models.

Installation
bash

pip install transformers

Example: Summarizing Text with Hugging Face
python

```python
from transformers import pipeline

# Initialize summarization pipeline
```

```
summarizer = pipeline("summarization")

# Input text
text = "Large Language Models have transformed the
way we analyze and understand data..."

# Generate summary
summary = summarizer(text, max_length=50,
min_length=10, do_sample=False)
print(summary[0]['summary_text'])
```

---

3. OpenAI
OpenAI provides API access to models like GPT-4, enabling natural language queries, data summarization, and automation.

Key Features
- **Fine-Tuned Models**:
  - Customize GPT models for domain-specific tasks.
- **Multilingual Support**:
  - Understands and generates text in multiple languages.
- **Ease of Integration**:
  - Works with REST APIs and SDKs.

Installation
bash

```
pip install openai
```

Example: Interacting with OpenAI API
python

```
import openai

# Set API key
openai.api_key = "your_api_key"

# Query the model
response = openai.Completion.create(
    model="text-davinci-003",
```

```python
    prompt="Summarize sales performance for Q2
2023.",
    max_tokens=100
)
print(response.choices[0].text.strip())
```

---

4. Pinecone
Pinecone is a vector database optimized for semantic search, allowing efficient querying and retrieval of relevant documents or data points.

Key Features
  - **Embedding Storage**:
      - Store high-dimensional embeddings for fast similarity searches.
  - **Scalable Infrastructure**:
      - Handle millions of vectors with low latency.
  - **Integration with LLMs**:
      - Works seamlessly with tools like Hugging Face and OpenAI.

Installation
bash

```
pip install pinecone-client
```

Example: Storing and Querying Embeddings
python

```python
import pinecone
from sentence_transformers import SentenceTransformer

# Initialize Pinecone
pinecone.init(api_key="your_pinecone_api_key",
environment="us-west1-gcp")

# Create a Pinecone index
index = pinecone.Index("llm-data")

# Generate embeddings
model = SentenceTransformer('all-MiniLM-L6-v2')
```

```
embeddings = model.encode(["This is a sales
document.", "This is a financial report."])

# Store embeddings
for i, emb in enumerate(embeddings):
    index.upsert([(str(i), emb)])

# Query the index
query_vector = model.encode(["Find similar documents
to sales."])
results = index.query(query_vector, top_k=1,
include_metadata=True)
print(results)
```

2.2.2 Using SQLAlchemy, Pandas, and Visualization Libraries
1. SQLAlchemy

SQLAlchemy is a Python library for interacting with databases. It provides an object-relational mapping (ORM) layer for easy query building and execution.

Key Features
- **Database Abstraction**:
    - Works with multiple databases, including MySQL, PostgreSQL, and SQLite.
- **Query Automation**:
    - Simplifies query creation using Python syntax.

Installation
bash

pip install sqlalchemy
Example: Querying a Database
python

```
from sqlalchemy import create_engine

# Connect to the database
engine = create_engine('sqlite:///sales.db')
```

```
# Query the database
query = "SELECT region, SUM(sales) AS total_sales
FROM sales_data GROUP BY region;"
with engine.connect() as connection:
    result = connection.execute(query)
    for row in result:
        print(row)
```

---

2. Pandas

Pandas is essential for data manipulation and analysis. It provides powerful tools for working with structured data, such as CSV files and SQL query results.

Key Features
- **DataFrames**:
    - Efficient tabular data structures.
- **Integration**:
    - Easily integrates with SQLAlchemy and visualization libraries.

Installation
bash

```
pip install pandas
```

Example: Data Analysis with Pandas
python

```
import pandas as pd

# Load sales data
data = pd.DataFrame({
    "Region": ["North", "South", "East", "West"],
    "Sales": [500000, 450000, 300000, 400000]
})

# Calculate total sales
total_sales = data["Sales"].sum()
print(f"Total Sales: ${total_sales}")
```

---

3. Visualization Libraries

Visualization is critical for interpreting and presenting data insights. Libraries like Matplotlib, Seaborn, and Plotly offer extensive capabilities.

3.1 Matplotlib

- **Use Case**: Simple static plots.
- **Installation**:

bash

```
pip install matplotlib
```

- **Example**:

python

```
import matplotlib.pyplot as plt

# Create a bar chart
regions = ["North", "South", "East", "West"]
sales = [500000, 450000, 300000, 400000]
plt.bar(regions, sales)
plt.title("Sales by Region")
plt.xlabel("Region")
plt.ylabel("Sales")
plt.show()
```

3.2 Plotly

- **Use Case**: Interactive visualizations.
- **Installation**:

bash

```
pip install plotly
```

- **Example**:

python

```
import plotly.express as px

# Interactive bar chart
data = {"Region": ["North", "South", "East", "West"],
"Sales": [500000, 450000, 300000, 400000]}
```

```
fig = px.bar(data, x="Region", y="Sales",
title="Interactive Sales by Region")
fig.show()
```

LangChain, Hugging Face, OpenAI, and Pinecone provide a robust foundation for building workflows around LLMs. When combined with SQLAlchemy, Pandas, and visualization libraries, they enable seamless data querying, manipulation, and presentation. These tools ensure a comprehensive and efficient environment for leveraging LLMs in data-centric applications. The next section will explore how to apply these tools in querying and interacting with structured data.

2.3 Accessing LLM APIs

Accessing Large Language Model (LLM) APIs is one of the most efficient ways to harness the power of advanced AI systems without managing complex infrastructure. Various API providers, such as OpenAI, Cohere, and Google, offer pre-trained models that can be integrated into workflows for querying, analyzing, and generating data insights. This section explains key providers and offers practical strategies for managing costs and optimizing API usage.

2.3.1 API Providers: OpenAI, Cohere, Google, and More

1. OpenAI
OpenAI provides API access to cutting-edge LLMs like GPT-4 and Codex, enabling natural language understanding, generation, and programming-related tasks.
Key Features
- **Models**: GPT-4, GPT-3.5, Codex (specialized for code).
- **Capabilities**:
  - Text summarization.
  - Language translation.
  - Data querying and analysis.
  - Programming assistance.
Pricing
- Usage-based pricing based on tokens processed.
  - **1 Token ≈ 4 Characters** (e.g., "The" = 1 token).

Example: Summarizing Data Insights
python

```python
import openai

# Set your API key
openai.api_key = "your_api_key"

# Query the model
response = openai.Completion.create(
    model="text-davinci-003",
    prompt="Summarize the sales trends in Q2 2023.",
    max_tokens=100
)
print(response.choices[0].text.strip())
```

2. Cohere
Cohere specializes in natural language processing and offers APIs for text generation, classification, and semantic search.

Key Features
- **Models**: Generation and classification models optimized for enterprise use.
- **Capabilities**:
    - Sentiment analysis.
    - Topic classification.
    - Semantic similarity.

Pricing
- Offers free and paid tiers with usage limits.

Example: Performing Sentiment Analysis
python

```python
import cohere

# Initialize the client
co = cohere.Client("your_api_key")
```

```
# Analyze sentiment
response = co.generate(
    model="command-xlarge",
    prompt="Analyze the sentiment of this text: 'The
product was amazing!'",
    max_tokens=50
)
print(response.generations[0].text.strip())
```

3. Google Cloud AI
Google offers API access to **PaLM 2** and other advanced language
models through its Vertex AI platform.

Key Features
- **Models**: PaLM 2 for text and chat applications.
- **Capabilities**:
  - Multilingual support.
  - Document summarization.
  - Data extraction.

Pricing
- Charges based on the number of characters processed.

Example: Using Google's Language Model
python

```
from google.cloud import aiplatform

# Initialize Vertex AI client
aiplatform.init(project="your_project_id")

# Request completion
response = aiplatform.generation.TextGeneration(
    model="text-bison",
    prompt="What are the top sales regions for
2023?",
    max_tokens=100
)
print(response.result)
```

4. Hugging Face
Hugging Face provides access to open-source models and APIs for tasks like text summarization, translation, and question answering.

Key Features
- **Models**: GPT-2, BERT, T5, and other fine-tuned models.
- **Capabilities**:
    - Text-to-text tasks.
    - Customizable pipelines.

Pricing
- Free access to open-source models; paid plans for enhanced performance.

Example: Summarizing Text
python

```
from transformers import pipeline

# Initialize summarization pipeline
summarizer = pipeline("summarization")

# Input text
text = "The sales data for Q2 shows a 20% growth in
the North region and a 15% decline in the East
region."

# Generate summary
summary = summarizer(text, max_length=50,
min_length=10, do_sample=False)
print(summary[0]['summary_text'])
```

5. Other Providers

Provider	Key Features	Use Cases
Anthropic	AI safety-focused LLMs (Claude).	Long-form text generation and ethical AI use.
Azure OpenAI	OpenAI integration with Azure cloud services.	Enterprise-grade AI deployments.
Aleph Alpha	Multimodal AI for text and image processing.	Research, summarization, and semantic search.

2.3.2 Managing Costs and Optimizing API Usage

Accessing LLM APIs often incurs costs based on usage, typically calculated by the number of tokens or characters processed. Effective cost management and optimization strategies are crucial for budget-friendly API integration.

1. Understanding Cost Structure
- **Token-Based Billing**:
  - OpenAI: Charges based on tokens processed in both input and output.
  - Example:
    - Input: *"Summarize sales trends."* (3 tokens).
    - Output: *"Sales are increasing in the North region."* (7 tokens).
    - Total Tokens: 10.
- **Tiered Pricing**:
  - Providers like Google and Cohere offer free tiers with limited usage, ideal for experimentation.

2. Strategies to Optimize API Usage
1. **Use Efficient Prompts**:
   - Minimize token usage by crafting concise and specific prompts.
   - Example:
     - Inefficient: *"Please analyze the sales data and explain the trends in detail for Q2."*
     - Efficient: *"Analyze Q2 sales trends."*
2. **Adjust Model Parameters**:
   - **Max Tokens**: Set a limit to prevent overly verbose outputs.
   - Example:

python

```
response = openai.Completion.create(
```

```
    model="text-davinci-003",
    prompt="Summarize Q2 sales.",
    max_tokens=50
)
```

3. **Leverage Caching**:
   - o Cache frequent queries locally to avoid redundant API calls.
   - o Example:

python

```
import pickle

# Cache response
cache = {}
query = "Summarize Q2 sales."
if query in cache:
    response = cache[query]
else:
    response = openai.Completion.create(prompt=query,
max_tokens=100)
    cache[query] = response
```

4. **Select Appropriate Models**:
   - o Use smaller or task-specific models for lightweight tasks.
   - o Example:
     - ▪ Use GPT-3.5 for general tasks instead of GPT-4 to save costs.
5. **Batch Requests**:
   - o Combine multiple prompts into a single request to reduce overhead.
   - o Example:

python

```
prompts = [
    "Summarize sales for Q2.",
    "List top-performing regions.",
    "Identify growth trends."
]
response = openai.Completion.create(
    model="text-davinci-003",
```

```
    prompt="\n".join(prompts),
    max_tokens=300
)
print(response.choices[0].text)
```

3. Monitor and Analyze Usage
Regular monitoring helps identify cost-heavy queries and optimize workflows.
- **Tools**:
  - OpenAI Usage Dashboard.
  - Custom monitoring scripts.

Example: Tracking Usage
python

```
import openai

# Monitor token usage
response = openai.Completion.create(
    model="text-davinci-003",
    prompt="Summarize Q2 sales trends.",
    max_tokens=50
)
tokens_used = response.usage.total_tokens
print(f"Tokens Used: {tokens_used}")
```

4. Fine-Tune Models Locally
Fine-tuning smaller models can reduce dependency on high-cost APIs for domain-specific tasks.
- Example: Fine-tune a Hugging Face model for summarizing financial reports.

5. Use Free or Open-Source Alternatives
- Experiment with open-source models like GPT-J or BERT for non-critical workflows.

Accessing LLM APIs from providers like OpenAI, Cohere, and Google unlocks powerful capabilities for data workflows. However, managing costs and optimizing usage are critical to maintaining efficiency and staying within budget. By implementing concise prompts, batching requests, and leveraging monitoring tools, you can maximize the value of these APIs while minimizing expenses. These strategies will ensure seamless integration of LLMs into your applications with cost-effectiveness and reliability.

2.4 Preparing Your Workspace

To effectively work with Large Language Models (LLMs) and data workflows, setting up a well-structured and organized workspace is essential. This section covers how to set up **Jupyter Notebooks** for experimentation and best practices for organizing your code and data files to ensure efficiency, reproducibility, and maintainability.

2.4.1 Setting Up Jupyter Notebooks for Experimentation
Why Use Jupyter Notebooks?
Jupyter Notebooks are an interactive development environment that allow you to write, test, and document code in a single interface. They are ideal for experimentation with LLMs and data workflows due to their flexibility and visualization capabilities.

1. Installing Jupyter Notebooks
Jupyter Notebooks can be installed as part of the Jupyter ecosystem or via data science distributions like Anaconda.
Installation via pip
    1. Activate your virtual environment:
bash

```
source env/bin/activate    # macOS/Linux
.\env\Scripts\activate     # Windows
```
    2. Install Jupyter:
bash

```
pip install notebook
```
    3. Verify installation:
bash

```
jupyter --version
```
Installation via Anaconda

1. Download and install [Anaconda](#).
2. Open the Anaconda Navigator and launch Jupyter Notebooks.

2. Launching Jupyter Notebooks

1. Navigate to your project directory in the terminal:

bash

```bash
cd path/to/your/project
```

2. Start Jupyter:

bash

```bash
jupyter notebook
```

3. Your default browser will open with the Jupyter Notebook interface, showing the files in your project directory.

3. Setting Up a Jupyter Notebook

Create a new notebook:

1. Click on the **New** button in the top-right corner and select **Python 3**.
2. Rename the notebook to reflect its purpose (e.g., Data_LLM_Experiment.ipynb).

4. Organizing Your Notebook
Structure of a Well-Organized Notebook

Section	Content
Title and Purpose	Use a Markdown cell to explain the notebook's objective.
Setup	Import libraries and configure the environment.
Data Loading	Load datasets or connect to APIs.
Analysis	Perform queries, data manipulation, and experiments with LLMs.
Results	Visualize and summarize findings.

Example Notebook Structure

markdown

```markdown
# Data Analysis with LLMs
```

This notebook demonstrates how to use GPT-4 to analyze sales data.

Setup
```python
# Import libraries
import openai
import pandas as pd
import matplotlib.pyplot as plt
Load Data
python

# Load sales data
data = pd.DataFrame({
    "Region": ["North", "South", "East", "West"],
    "Sales": [500000, 450000, 300000, 400000]
})
data.head()
Analyze Data
python

# Use GPT-4 to summarize sales trends
openai.api_key = "your_api_key"
response = openai.Completion.create(
    model="text-davinci-003",
    prompt="Summarize the sales trends in this dataset: " + str(data),
    max_tokens=100
)
print(response.choices[0].text.strip())
```

---

5. Enhancing Productivity in Jupyter
1. **Use Markdown for Documentation**:
   - Clearly document each step of the workflow.
   - Example:

markdown

Step 1: Load Sales Data
The dataset includes sales performance for different regions.

2. **Install Useful Extensions**:
   - ○ Install **Jupyter Notebook Extensions** for additional features:

bash

```
pip install jupyter_contrib_nbextensions
jupyter contrib nbextension install --user
```

   - ○ Enable extensions like Table of Contents and Code Folding.
3. **Keyboard Shortcuts**:
   - ○ **Run Cell**: Shift + Enter
   - ○ **Insert Cell Below**: B
   - ○ **Delete Cell**: DD

2.4.2 Best Practices for Organizing Code and Data Files

Proper organization of code and data files ensures that projects are easy to manage, debug, and share. This is especially important in collaborative or long-term projects.

---

1. Directory Structure

A well-organized project directory separates raw data, processed data, code, and documentation.

Recommended Directory Structure
plaintext

```
project_name/
├── notebooks/      # Jupyter Notebooks
├── data/           # Data files
│   ├── raw/        # Raw datasets
│   ├── processed/  # Cleaned/processed data
├── src/            # Python scripts
├── models/         # Machine learning or LLM-related models
├── output/         # Results (charts, summaries, etc.)
├── requirements.txt # List of required libraries
├── README.md       # Project overview and setup instructions
```

Example: Directory for an LLM Project
plaintext

```
data_llm_project/
├── notebooks/
│   ├── analysis.ipynb
├── data/
│   ├── raw/
│   │   ├── sales_data.csv
│   ├── processed/
│       ├── cleaned_sales_data.csv
├── src/
│   ├── query_llm.py
│   ├── process_data.py
├── models/
│   ├── fine_tuned_gpt4/
├── output/
│   ├── sales_summary.png
│   ├── trends_report.txt
├── requirements.txt
├── README.md
```

2. Naming Conventions

1. **Files**:
   - Use clear, descriptive names.
   - Example: sales_data.csv instead of data1.csv.
2. **Variables**:
   - Use descriptive names in code.
   - Example:

python

```python
total_sales = data["Sales"].sum()
```

3. **Scripts**:
   - Name scripts based on functionality.
   - Example: query_llm.py for LLM-related queries.

3. Version Control

Use Git for version control to track changes and collaborate effectively.

Steps to Initialize a Git Repository

1. Initialize:

bash

```
git init
```

2. Add Files:

bash

```
git add .
```

3. Commit Changes:

bash

```
git commit -m "Initial commit"
```

4. Push to a Remote Repository (e.g., GitHub):

bash

```
git remote add origin <repository_url>
git push -u origin main
```

---

4. Documentation

1. **README.md**:
   - Provide an overview of the project and setup instructions.
   - Example:

markdown

```
# Data LLM Project
This project uses GPT-4 to analyze sales data.

## Setup
1. Install dependencies:
   ```bash
   pip install -r requirements.txt
```

2. Run the analysis notebook:

bash

```
jupyter notebook notebooks/analysis.ipynb
```
```

2. **Comments in Code**:
   - o   Include clear comments to explain functionality.
   - o   Example:

python

```
# Summarize sales data using GPT-4
response = openai.Completion.create(
    model="text-davinci-003",
    prompt="Summarize sales trends",
    max_tokens=100
)
```

5. Backup and Data Security
1. **Cloud Storage**:
   - o   Use platforms like Google Drive, Dropbox, or AWS S3 to back up important data.
2. **Sensitive Data**:
   - o   Avoid storing sensitive API keys or credentials in code. Use environment variables instead:

python

```
import os
api_key = os.getenv("OPENAI_API_KEY")
```

Preparing your workspace with Jupyter Notebooks and a well-organized file structure lays the foundation for productive and reproducible workflows. By following these best practices, you'll create an efficient environment for experimenting with LLMs and managing data-centric projects. This preparation ensures smooth progress as you tackle increasingly complex tasks in the following chapters

2.5 Key Takeaways

The previous sections in this chapter explored the essential tools, frameworks, and best practices for setting up your workspace for working with Large Language Models (LLMs). This section consolidates the key learnings into a **comprehensive tools checklist** and highlights the critical steps required to prepare an effective development environment.

2.5.1 Tools Checklist and Setup Essentials
Overview
Working with LLMs requires a well-configured environment that integrates libraries, APIs, and utilities for seamless experimentation and production workflows. A properly set up environment ensures efficiency, reproducibility, and scalability.

1. Tools Checklist
The following checklist summarizes the key tools and libraries discussed throughout this chapter, organized by their purpose:

Core Tools and Frameworks

Tool	Purpose	Installation Command
Python 3.8+	Programming language for LLM workflows.	Python Download
Jupyter	Interactive notebooks for experimentation.	pip install notebook

LLM Integration

Tool	Purpose	Installation Command
OpenAI	Access GPT models via API.	pip install openai
Hugging Face	Open-source models and transformers.	pip install transformers
LangChain	Workflow management and chaining prompts.	pip install langchain

Tool	Purpose	Installation Command
Cohere	Text generation and classification APIs.	pip install cohere

Data Manipulation and Analysis

Tool	Purpose	Installation Command
Pandas	Data manipulation and analysis.	pip install pandas
NumPy	Numerical computations.	pip install numpy

Database Access

Tool	Purpose	Installation Command
SQLAlchemy	Query and manage relational databases.	pip install sqlalchemy

Visualization

Tool	Purpose	Installation Command
Matplotlib	Create static plots and charts.	pip install matplotlib
Plotly	Build interactive visualizations.	pip install plotly

Version Control

Tool	Purpose	Installation Command
Git	Track and manage code changes.	Git Download

2. Setup Essentials

Below are the critical steps to set up your environment for LLM workflows:

Step 1: Install Python and Jupyter

- Ensure Python 3.8 or higher is installed. Install Jupyter for interactive notebook support.
- Verify installation:

bash

```
python --version
jupyter --version
```

Step 2: Set Up Virtual Environment

- Create a virtual environment to isolate dependencies:

bash

```
python -m venv env
source env/bin/activate   # macOS/Linux
.\env\Scripts\activate    # Windows
```

Step 3: Install Required Libraries
- Use the provided tools checklist to install all necessary libraries:

bash

```
pip install notebook openai transformers langchain
cohere pandas matplotlib plotly
```

Step 4: Configure API Access
- Set up API keys for services like OpenAI and Cohere:
  - Store keys in environment variables for security:

bash

```
export OPENAI_API_KEY="your_openai_key"
export COHERE_API_KEY="your_cohere_key"
```

Step 5: Organize Workspace
- Follow the recommended directory structure:

plaintext

```
project_name/
├── notebooks/          # Jupyter notebooks
├── data/               # Raw and processed datasets
├── src/                # Python scripts
├── output/             # Results (e.g., charts,
reports)
├── requirements.txt    # List of dependencies
├── README.md           # Project overview
Step 6: Verify Installations
Create a script to verify key library installations:
python

import openai
import pandas as pd
import matplotlib.pyplot as plt
```

```
print("All required libraries are installed and
working.")
```

---

3. Optimizing Workflow
Using Jupyter Notebooks
- Structure notebooks for clarity:
  - Include sections for setup, data loading, analysis, and results.
  - Use Markdown cells to document your process.

Managing Dependencies
- Save dependencies in a requirements.txt file:

bash

```
pip freeze > requirements.txt
```
- Recreate the environment:

bash

```
pip install -r requirements.txt
```
Version Control
- Use Git to track changes:

bash

```
git init
git add .
git commit -m "Initial commit"
```

Backup and Data Security
- Use cloud storage or version control to back up important files.
- Avoid hardcoding sensitive information like API keys in scripts.

---

4. Common Errors and Troubleshooting
Error: Missing Dependencies
- **Cause**: Required libraries not installed.
- **Solution**: Install missing packages:

bash

```
pip install <missing_package>
```
Error: API Key Not Found

- **Cause**: API key not set in environment variables.
- **Solution**:

bash

```
export OPENAI_API_KEY="your_key"
```

Error: Jupyter Not Launching
- **Cause**: Jupyter Notebook not installed or environment not activated.
- **Solution**:

bash

```
pip install notebook
source env/bin/activate
jupyter notebook
```

5. Summary of Tools by Purpose

Category	Recommended Tools
LLM Interaction	OpenAI, Hugging Face, LangChain, Cohere
Data Analysis	Pandas, NumPy
Database Access	SQLAlchemy
Visualization	Matplotlib, Plotly
Experimentation	Jupyter Notebooks
Version Control	Git

This section has consolidated the tools and setup essentials required for effective LLM workflows. By following the tools checklist and setup steps, you'll have a robust and organized environment ready for experimentation and production. This foundational preparation ensures that you can seamlessly work with LLMs, manage data efficiently, and scale your projects with confidence.

Chapter 3: Querying Data with Natural Language

Querying data using natural language is one of the most transformative applications of Large Language Models (LLMs). By translating natural language inputs into SQL queries, LLMs enable users to interact with databases without requiring technical knowledge of SQL syntax. This chapter focuses on the basics of query translation and the art of prompt engineering for effective and accurate query generation.

3.1 Natural Language to SQL

Natural Language to SQL (NL2SQL) systems empower non-technical users to retrieve and analyze data using plain language. With LLMs, these systems become accessible, flexible, and powerful.

3.1.1 Basics of Query Translation

The process of converting a natural language query into an SQL statement involves understanding the intent of the query, identifying the relevant tables and fields, and constructing a syntactically correct SQL query.

How Query Translation Works

1. **Input**:
   - Natural language query provided by the user.
   - Example: *"Show total sales by region for Q2 2023."*
2. **Processing**:
   - The model interprets the query, identifies the relevant data fields (e.g., "sales," "region"), and applies filters (e.g., "Q2 2023").
   - Constructs an SQL query:

sql

```
SELECT region, SUM(sales) AS total_sales
FROM sales_data
WHERE quarter = 'Q2' AND year = 2023
GROUP BY region;
```

3. **Output**:
   - o Executable SQL query that retrieves the requested data.

Components of SQL Translation

Component	Description
Table Identification	Identifies the table(s) to query (e.g., sales_data).
Field Mapping	Maps natural language fields (e.g., "sales") to database columns (sales).
Filters and Conditions	Translates constraints like time ranges (Q2 2023) into SQL WHERE clauses.
Aggregations	Converts operations like "total sales" into SQL functions (e.g., SUM).

Code Example: Basic NL2SQL Conversion
python

```python
import openai

# Set API key
openai.api_key = "your_openai_key"

# Natural language query
nl_query = "Show total sales by region for Q2 2023."

# Translate using OpenAI
response = openai.Completion.create(
    model="text-davinci-003",
    prompt=f"Translate this into SQL: {nl_query}",
    max_tokens=100
)

# SQL query output
```

```
print(response.choices[0].text.strip())
Output:
sql

SELECT region, SUM(sales) AS total_sales
FROM sales_data
WHERE quarter = 'Q2' AND year = 2023
GROUP BY region;
```

Challenges in Query Translation

Challenge	Description	Solution
Ambiguity	Natural language queries can be vague or open to interpretation.	Clarify queries with follow-up prompts.
Complex Joins	Multi-table queries require understanding relationships between tables.	Provide metadata or schema information as context.
Field Name Mismatch	Field names in the database may differ from natural language terms.	Use aliases or mappings to bridge the gap.
Context Awareness	The query may depend on previous interactions or implied context.	Maintain state across interactions using conversational history.

Schema Information in Query Translation

Providing schema information ensures the LLM generates accurate SQL queries.

Schema Example

plaintext

Table: sales_data
Columns:
- region (TEXT)
- sales (INTEGER)
- quarter (TEXT)

- year (INTEGER)
Prompt with Schema:
python

```
prompt = """
Table schema:
- Table name: sales_data
- Columns: region (TEXT), sales (INTEGER), quarter (TEXT), year
(INTEGER)

Translate the following natural language query into SQL:
'Show total sales by region for Q2 2023.'
"""
response = openai.Completion.create(
    model="text-davinci-003",
    prompt=prompt,
    max_tokens=100
)
print(response.choices[0].text.strip())
```

3.1.2 Understanding Prompt Engineering for Queries
Prompt engineering is the practice of crafting effective input prompts to guide the LLM in generating accurate and relevant SQL queries.

Importance of Prompt Engineering
1. **Clarity**:
    o   A well-structured prompt minimizes ambiguity, improving output quality.
2. **Context**:
    o   Providing schema or example queries ensures the model generates outputs aligned with the database.
3. **Flexibility**:
    o   Structured prompts allow the model to handle diverse and complex queries.

Key Strategies for Prompt Engineering

1. **Provide Schema Information**:
   - Clearly define table names, columns, and data types.
   - Example:

python

```
prompt = """
Table schema:
- Table name: sales_data
- Columns: region (TEXT), sales (INTEGER), quarter
(TEXT), year (INTEGER)

Translate the following query:
'Show total sales for each region in 2023.'
"""
```

2. **Use Example Queries**:
   - Include examples to set expectations for format and logic.
   - Example:

python

```
prompt = """
Example queries:
- Input: 'Show total sales by region for 2022.'
  SQL: SELECT region, SUM(sales) AS total_sales FROM
sales_data WHERE year = 2022 GROUP BY region;

Translate: 'List average sales for Q1 2023.'
"""
```

3. **Guide the Model**:
   - Specify constraints or output formats to align with requirements.
   - Example:

python

```
prompt = """
Translate the following query into SQL. Use 'AS' for
aliases and ensure proper GROUP BY clauses.
Query: 'Find the total revenue in 2023 for each
region.'
"""
```

Refining Prompts for Better Outputs

Issue	Weak Prompt	Refined Prompt
Ambiguity	"Get sales data."	"Get total sales by region for Q2 2023."
Missing Schema	"Show total sales."	"Use the table sales_data with columns region, sales, year."
Output Format	"Write a query."	"Write a SQL query in proper syntax with column aliases."

Advanced Prompt Engineering with Few-Shot Learning

Few-shot learning involves providing the model with a few examples to guide its behavior.

Few-Shot Prompt Example

python

```
prompt = """
Table schema:
- Table name: sales_data
- Columns: region (TEXT), sales (INTEGER), quarter
(TEXT), year (INTEGER)

Examples:
1. Input: 'Show total sales by region for Q2 2022.'
   SQL: SELECT region, SUM(sales) AS total_sales FROM sales_data
WHERE quarter = 'Q2' AND year = 2022 GROUP BY region;

2. Input: 'List average sales by quarter for 2023.'
   SQL: SELECT quarter, AVG(sales) AS avg_sales FROM sales_data
WHERE year = 2023 GROUP BY quarter;

Translate: 'Find total revenue for Q2 2023.'
"""
response = openai.Completion.create(
    model="text-davinci-003",
    prompt=prompt,
```

```
    max_tokens=100
)
print(response.choices[0].text.strip())
```

This section introduced the basics of translating natural language to SQL using LLMs and the critical role of prompt engineering in ensuring accurate results. By combining schema information, examples, and well-structured prompts, users can unlock the full potential of LLMs to query data efficiently and effectively. As we progress, we will explore more advanced query techniques and real-world use cases for NL2SQL systems.

3.2 Working with Structured Data

Structured data is the backbone of data analysis in relational databases. It consists of well-organized, tabular datasets that can be queried using SQL. LLMs enhance the process by allowing users to craft queries in natural language, which are then translated into SQL. This section delves into simple and complex query techniques and demonstrates real-world use cases for automating data requests.

3.2.1 Simple Queries: Selection, Filtering, and Sorting
1. Selection
Selection involves retrieving specific columns or rows from a table.
Example: Retrieving Columns
- **Natural Language Query**: "List all regions and their sales."
- **SQL Query**:

sql

```sql
SELECT region, sales
FROM sales_data;
```
Code Example: Translating and Executing
python

```python
import pandas as pd

# Sample data
data = pd.DataFrame({
    "Region": ["North", "South", "East", "West"],
```

```
    "Sales": [500000, 450000, 300000, 400000],
    "Year": [2023, 2023, 2023, 2023]
})

# Display selected columns
selected_columns = data[["Region", "Sales"]]
print(selected_columns)
```

Output:

mathematica

```
  Region  Sales
0  North  500000
1  South  450000
2   East  300000
3   West  400000
```

---

2. Filtering

Filtering narrows down data based on specific conditions using the WHERE clause.

Example: Filtering Rows

- **Natural Language Query**: "Show sales for the North region in 2023."
- **SQL Query**:

sql

```
SELECT region, sales
FROM sales_data
WHERE region = 'North' AND year = 2023;
```

Code Example: Filtering Rows

python

```
# Filter rows based on conditions
filtered_data = data[(data["Region"] == "North") &
(data["Year"] == 2023)]
print(filtered_data)
```

Output:

mathematica

```
   Region  Sales  Year
0  North  500000  2023
```

---

3. Sorting

Sorting organizes data in ascending or descending order using the ORDER BY clause.

Example: Sorting by Sales

- **Natural Language Query**: "List all regions sorted by sales in descending order."
- **SQL Query**:

sql

```sql
SELECT region, sales
FROM sales_data
ORDER BY sales DESC;
```

Code Example: Sorting

python

```python
# Sort data by sales
sorted_data = data.sort_values(by="Sales",
ascending=False)
print(sorted_data)
```

Output:

yaml

```
   Region  Sales  Year
0  North  500000  2023
1  South  450000  2023
3  West   400000  2023
2  East   300000  2023
```

3.2.2 Complex Queries: Joins, Aggregations, and Subqueries

1. Joins

Joins combine data from multiple tables based on a related column.

Example: Inner Join

- **Natural Language Query**: "Combine sales data with region details."
- **SQL Query**:

sql

```sql
SELECT sales_data.region, sales_data.sales, region_details.manager
FROM sales_data
INNER JOIN region_details
ON sales_data.region = region_details.region;
```

Code Example: Performing a Join

python

```python
# Sample datasets
sales_data = pd.DataFrame({
    "Region": ["North", "South", "East", "West"],
    "Sales": [500000, 450000, 300000, 400000]
})
region_details = pd.DataFrame({
    "Region": ["North", "South", "East", "West"],
    "Manager": ["Alice", "Bob", "Charlie", "Diana"]
})

# Perform join
joined_data = pd.merge(sales_data, region_details, on="Region")
print(joined_data)
```

Output:

mathematica

```
   Region  Sales   Manager
0  North   500000  Alice
1  South   450000  Bob
2  East    300000  Charlie
3  West    400000  Diana
```

---

2. Aggregations

Aggregations summarize data using functions like SUM, AVG, COUNT, etc.

Example: Total Sales by Region

- **Natural Language Query**: "Find total sales for each region."
- **SQL Query**:

sql

```sql
SELECT region, SUM(sales) AS total_sales
FROM sales_data
GROUP BY region;
```

Code Example: Aggregations

python

```python
# Aggregate total sales by region
total_sales = sales_data.groupby("Region").sum()
print(total_sales)
```

Output:

markdown

```
        Sales
Region
East    300000
North   500000
South   450000
West    400000
```

---

3. Subqueries

Subqueries are nested queries used to filter or process data.

Example: Top Region by Sales

- **Natural Language Query**: "Find the region with the highest sales."
- **SQL Query**:

sql

```sql
SELECT region
FROM sales_data
WHERE sales = (SELECT MAX(sales) FROM sales_data);
```

Code Example: Subqueries

python

```python
# Identify the region with the highest sales
top_region = sales_data[sales_data["Sales"] ==
sales_data["Sales"].max()]
print(top_region)
```

Output:
mathematica

```
   Region  Sales
0  North   500000
```

3.2.3 Real-World Examples: Automating Data Requests
In real-world scenarios, LLMs can automate data retrieval tasks, making them accessible to non-technical users.

Example 1: Generating SQL Queries Dynamically
Use Case:
A business user asks: "Show me total sales for each region in 2023."
Code Example: Automating Query Translation
python

```
import openai

# Define schema and user query
schema = """
Table schema:
- Table name: sales_data
- Columns: region (TEXT), sales (INTEGER), year
(INTEGER)
"""

user_query = "Show me total sales for each region in
2023."

# Use OpenAI to generate SQL
response = openai.Completion.create(
    model="text-davinci-003",
    prompt=f"{schema}\nTranslate the following query
to SQL:\n'{user_query}'",
    max_tokens=100
)
print(response.choices[0].text.strip())
```
Output:
sql

```sql
SELECT region, SUM(sales) AS total_sales
FROM sales_data
WHERE year = 2023
GROUP BY region;
```

Example 2: Automating Insights

Use Case:

A manager asks: "What were the top three regions by sales last year?"

Code Example: Automating Insight Extraction

python

```python
# Sample dataset
data = pd.DataFrame({
    "Region": ["North", "South", "East", "West"],
    "Sales": [500000, 450000, 300000, 400000],
    "Year": [2022, 2022, 2022, 2022]
})

# Extract top 3 regions by sales
top_regions = data.nlargest(3, "Sales")
print(top_regions)
```

Output:

yaml

```
  Region  Sales  Year
0  North  500000  2022
1  South  450000  2022
3  West   400000  2022
```

Example 3: Interactive Chat for Data Requests

Use Case:

Enable users to interact with data through a chatbot.

Code Example: LLM-Powered Chatbot

python

```python
# User input
user_query = "What are the total sales for 2023?"

# Generate SQL and execute
```

```python
response = openai.Completion.create(
    model="text-davinci-003",
    prompt=f"{schema}\nTranslate the following query
to SQL:\n'{user_query}'",
    max_tokens=100
)
sql_query = response.choices[0].text.strip()

# Execute SQL on pandas dataframe
total_sales = data[data["Year"] ==
2023]["Sales"].sum()
print(f"Total Sales for 2023: ${total_sales}")
```
Output:
bash

Total Sales for 2023: $1,650,000

This section provided a comprehensive exploration of querying structured data using LLMs, covering simple queries (selection, filtering, sorting), complex queries (joins, aggregations, subqueries), and real-world automation examples. By mastering these techniques, you can efficiently transform natural language queries into actionable insights, bridging the gap between technical and non-technical users. The next section will delve deeper into leveraging LLMs for data analysis and visualization.

3.3 Handling Semi-Structured Data

Semi-structured data, such as JSON, XML, and CSV files, occupies a middle ground between structured relational data and unstructured data. Unlike structured data, semi-structured data does not conform to a strict schema but contains tags or markers to separate elements. Querying and transforming this data effectively is crucial for seamless integration into data workflows. In this section, we explore how to handle semi-structured data and automate parsing and transformation tasks using modern tools and Large Language Models (LLMs).

3.3.1 Querying JSON, XML, and CSV Files

Semi-structured data is prevalent in APIs, configuration files, and exported data formats. Tools like Python's pandas for CSVs, json for JSON files, and xml.etree.ElementTree for XML files simplify querying and processing.

---

1. Querying JSON Files

JSON (JavaScript Object Notation) is a lightweight, human-readable format commonly used for data exchange.

Example JSON File

json

```json
{
  "sales": [
    {"region": "North", "sales": 500000, "year": 2023},
    {"region": "South", "sales": 450000, "year": 2023},
    {"region": "East", "sales": 300000, "year": 2023},
    {"region": "West", "sales": 400000, "year": 2023}
  ]
}
```

Code Example: Querying JSON

python

```python
import json

# Load JSON data
with open('sales_data.json', 'r') as file:
    data = json.load(file)

# Extract sales for the North region
north_sales = [item for item in data['sales'] if
item['region'] == 'North']
print(north_sales)
```

Output:

json

```
[{"region": "North", "sales": 500000, "year": 2023}]
```

2. Querying XML Files

XML (Extensible Markup Language) is often used for data storage and transport in hierarchical structures.

Example XML File

xml

```xml
<sales>
    <entry>
        <region>North</region>
        <sales>500000</sales>
        <year>2023</year>
    </entry>
    <entry>
        <region>South</region>
        <sales>450000</sales>
        <year>2023</year>
    </entry>
</sales>
```

Code Example: Querying XML

python

```python
import xml.etree.ElementTree as ET

# Parse XML data
tree = ET.parse('sales_data.xml')
root = tree.getroot()

# Extract sales for the North region
for entry in root.findall('entry'):
    region = entry.find('region').text
    sales = entry.find('sales').text
    if region == 'North':
        print(f"Region: {region}, Sales: {sales}")
```

Output:
yaml

```
Region: North, Sales: 500000
```

3. Querying CSV Files

CSV (Comma-Separated Values) is a tabular format widely used for storing structured and semi-structured data.

Example CSV File

csv

```
Region,Sales,Year
North,500000,2023
South,450000,2023
East,300000,2023
West,400000,2023
```

Code Example: Querying CSV

python

```
import pandas as pd

# Load CSV data
data = pd.read_csv('sales_data.csv')

# Filter data for the North region
north_sales = data[data['Region'] == 'North']
print(north_sales)
```

Output:

mathematica

```
  Region  Sales  Year
0  North  500000  2023
```

3.3.2 Automating Data Parsing and Transformation

Automation is essential for handling semi-structured data efficiently. Tools like LLMs can assist by generating scripts, interpreting schemas, and suggesting transformations.

1. Automating JSON Parsing
Example: Summarizing JSON Data

A user asks: "Summarize total sales by region from this JSON file."
Code Example: Automating Summary
python

```
import json

# Load JSON data
with open('sales_data.json', 'r') as file:
    data = json.load(file)

# Summarize sales by region
summary = {item['region']: item['sales'] for item in
data['sales']}
print(summary)
```

Output:
json

```
{"North": 500000, "South": 450000, "East": 300000, "West": 400000}
```

---

2. Automating XML Parsing
Example: Transforming XML to CSV
Convert the XML sales data into a CSV file for easier analysis.
Code Example: XML to CSV
python

```
import xml.etree.ElementTree as ET
import csv

# Parse XML data
tree = ET.parse('sales_data.xml')
root = tree.getroot()

# Write to CSV
with open('sales_data.csv', 'w', newline='') as
csvfile:
   writer = csv.writer(csvfile)
    writer.writerow(['Region', 'Sales', 'Year'])
    for entry in root.findall('entry'):
```

```python
        region = entry.find('region').text
        sales = entry.find('sales').text
        year = entry.find('year').text
        writer.writerow([region, sales, year])
```

Result:

csv

```
Region,Sales,Year
North,500000,2023
South,450000,2023
East,300000,2023
West,400000,2023
```

---

3. Automating CSV Parsing
Example: Generating Insights from CSV
A user asks: "Which region had the highest sales?"
Code Example: Analyzing CSV Data
python

```python
import pandas as pd

# Load CSV data
data = pd.read_csv('sales_data.csv')

# Identify the region with the highest sales
top_region = data.loc[data['Sales'].idxmax()]
print(f"Top Region: {top_region['Region']}, Sales:
{top_region['Sales']}")
```

Output:

mathematica

```
Top Region: North, Sales: 500000
```

---

4. Using LLMs to Automate Parsing and Transformation
Example: Automating Data Parsing with OpenAI
A user asks: "Write a script to convert JSON sales data into a pandas DataFrame."
Code Example: Using LLMs
python

```python
import openai

# User prompt
prompt = "Write a Python script to load JSON sales
data and convert it into a pandas DataFrame."

# Query OpenAI API
response = openai.Completion.create(
    model="text-davinci-003",
    prompt=prompt,
    max_tokens=150
)
print(response.choices[0].text.strip())
Generated Output:
python
```

```python
import json
import pandas as pd

# Load JSON data
with open('sales_data.json', 'r') as file:
    data = json.load(file)

# Convert to pandas DataFrame
df = pd.DataFrame(data['sales'])
print(df)
```

---

5. Automating Transformations Across Formats
Example: Transform JSON to SQL Table
A user asks: "Transform this JSON data into an SQL insert statement."
Code Example: JSON to SQL
python

```python
# Load JSON data
with open('sales_data.json', 'r') as file:
    data = json.load(file)

# Generate SQL insert statements
```

```python
insert_statements = []
for item in data['sales']:
    statement = f"INSERT INTO sales_data (region,
sales, year) VALUES ('{item['region']}',
{item['sales']}, {item['year']});"
    insert_statements.append(statement)

# Print SQL statements
for stmt in insert_statements:
    print(stmt)
```
Output:
sql

INSERT INTO sales_data (region, sales, year) VALUES ('North',
500000, 2023);
INSERT INTO sales_data (region, sales, year) VALUES ('South',
450000, 2023);
INSERT INTO sales_data (region, sales, year) VALUES ('East', 300000,
2023);
INSERT INTO sales_data (region, sales, year) VALUES ('West', 400000,
2023);

Handling semi-structured data such as JSON, XML, and CSV files requires specialized tools and workflows. By leveraging Python libraries and automation techniques, you can parse, query, and transform semi-structured data efficiently. Additionally, LLMs can assist in generating scripts and automating repetitive tasks, bridging the gap between raw data and actionable insights. This capability makes them invaluable for modern data workflows

3.4 Challenges and Pitfalls

While querying structured and semi-structured data with Large Language Models (LLMs) is transformative, it is not without challenges. Ambiguous user queries and errors in LLM-generated queries can lead to inefficiencies or incorrect results. This section addresses these challenges and provides strategies for clarifying ambiguous queries and implementing robust error handling mechanisms.

3.4.1 Ambiguous Queries and How to Clarify Them

Ambiguity arises when a natural language query lacks specificity, making it difficult for the LLM to accurately interpret the user's intent. This can lead to incomplete, irrelevant, or incorrect results.

---

1. Understanding Ambiguity in Queries

Common Sources of Ambiguity
1. **Vague Descriptions**:
   - Query: "Show me sales data."
   - Ambiguity: Which sales data? For which regions or time periods?
2. **Lack of Context**:
   - Query: "List top-performing regions."
   - Ambiguity: What is the metric for performance? Sales? Revenue growth?
3. **Multiple Interpretations**:
   - Query: "Filter out bad regions."
   - Ambiguity: What defines a "bad" region? Low sales? Negative growth?
4. **Implied Assumptions**:
   - Query: "Find last year's total revenue."
   - Ambiguity: Does "last year" mean the most recent fiscal year or calendar year?

---

2. Strategies to Clarify Ambiguity

1. Prompt Refinement

Encourage the user to refine their query with specific details.

Example: Handling Vagueness
- **Original Query**: "Show me sales data."
- **Refined Prompt**: "Can you specify the region, year, or product for the sales data?"

Code Example: Prompt Refinement

python

```
def clarify_query(user_query):
```

```python
    if "sales data" in user_query:
        return "Could you specify which region, year,
or product category you are interested in?"
    return "Query seems clear."

# Test the function
print(clarify_query("Show me sales data."))
```
Output:
sql

Could you specify which region, year, or product category you are interested in?

---

2. Schema Guidance
Provide users with schema details to help frame their queries.
Example:
- **Schema**:

plaintext

Table: sales_data
Columns: region, sales, product, year
- **Clarified Query**: "List sales for the North region by product in 2023."

3. Follow-Up Questions
Use conversational systems to request additional details.
Example:
- **User Query**: "List top-performing regions."
- **Follow-Up**: "Should I use total sales or revenue growth as the performance metric?"

---

4. LLM-Assisted Clarification
LLMs can generate clarifying questions dynamically.
Code Example: Generating Follow-Up Questions
python

```python
import openai
```

```
# User query
user_query = "List top-performing regions."

# Prompt LLM for clarification
response = openai.Completion.create(
    model="text-davinci-003",
    prompt=f"Suggest clarifying questions for the
query: '{user_query}'",
    max_tokens=50
)
print(response.choices[0].text.strip())
Output:
css
```

What metric should I use to determine top-performing regions? Sales, profit, or revenue growth?

---

3. Examples of Resolving Ambiguity
Scenario 1: Vague Query
- **Query**: "Show me the data for Q2."
- **Resolution**: Clarify which dataset or metrics (e.g., sales, revenue, expenses).

Scenario 2: Context Misalignment
- **Query**: "What is the growth rate?"
- **Resolution**: Specify whether to calculate growth based on sales, revenue, or another field.

Scenario 3: Imprecise Metrics
- **Query**: "List underperforming regions."
- **Resolution**: Define "underperforming" (e.g., below 20% revenue growth).

3.4.2 Error Handling in LLM-Generated Queries
Even with well-constructed prompts, LLMs can produce errors in SQL queries due to incorrect logic, syntax issues, or misinterpretations of schema.

1. Common Errors in LLM-Generated Queries
1. Syntax Errors
Generated SQL queries may include invalid syntax.

- **Example**:

sql

```
SELECT region, sales
FROM sales_data
WHERE year == 2023;  -- Incorrect syntax
```

2. Field Name Mismatches
Field names in the SQL query may not match the actual database schema.

- **Example**:

sql

```
SELECT region_name, sales
FROM sales_data;  -- Field 'region_name' does not exist
```

3. Logical Errors
The query logic may not align with the user's intent.

- **Example**:
    - Intent: "Show average sales."
    - Error: Generates SUM(sales) instead of AVG(sales).

4. Missing Filters
The query omits necessary conditions.

- **Example**:

sql

```
SELECT region, sales
FROM sales_data;  -- Missing WHERE clause for specific year
```

2. Strategies for Robust Error Handling
1. Schema Validation

Validate generated SQL queries against the database schema before execution.

Code Example: Validating Field Names

python

```python
def validate_query_fields(query, schema):
    schema_columns = schema["columns"]
    for field in query.split():
        if field in schema_columns:
            continue
        elif field.startswith("SELECT") or
field.startswith("FROM"):
            continue
        else:
            return f"Invalid field: {field}"
    return "Query is valid."

# Example schema
schema = {"columns": ["region", "sales", "year"]}

# Test the validation function
print(validate_query_fields("SELECT region,
total_sales FROM sales_data", schema))
```

Output:
yaml

Invalid field: total_sales

---

2. Error Feedback Loops
Capture error messages from the database and prompt the LLM for corrections.

Code Example: Handling SQL Errors
python

```python
import sqlite3

# Sample database connection
connection = sqlite3.connect(':memory:')
```

```
# Sample query with error
query = "SELECT region_name, sales FROM sales_data;"

try:
    cursor = connection.cursor()
    cursor.execute(query)
except sqlite3.OperationalError as e:
    print(f"SQL Error: {e}")
```
Output:
sql

SQL Error: no such column: region_name

---

3. Query Testing
Test LLM-generated queries in a sandbox environment to detect and fix errors before running on production data.

---

4. Error-Aware Prompting
Instruct the LLM to include error checks in its output.
Prompt Example:
- **Input**: "Generate SQL to list total sales by region in 2023 and include error checks."
- **Output**:
sql

```sql
SELECT region, SUM(sales) AS total_sales
FROM sales_data
WHERE year = 2023
GROUP BY region;

-- Error Check: Ensure 'region' and 'sales' exist in the schema
```

---

3. Examples of Error Handling
Scenario 1: Syntax Error
- **Error**: == instead of =.
- **Solution**: Regex or programmatic correction.
python

```
corrected_query = query.replace("==", "=")
```
Scenario 2: Missing Filters
- **Error**: No WHERE clause.
- **Solution**: Add default filters for ambiguous queries.

Scenario 3: Logical Error
- **Error**: Incorrect aggregation function.
- **Solution**: Use follow-up LLM prompt to validate logic.

Handling ambiguous queries and errors in LLM-generated SQL is crucial for reliable data workflows. By refining prompts, validating schemas, and implementing robust error-handling strategies, users can mitigate common pitfalls and ensure accurate query generation. These practices not only improve the reliability of LLM-powered systems but also enhance user trust and productivity

3.5 Interactive Exercise: Building an LLM-Powered Query Assistant

Interactive query assistants powered by Large Language Models (LLMs) enable users to access and analyze data using natural language. This exercise provides a step-by-step guide to build a basic LLM-powered query assistant capable of understanding natural language inputs, translating them into SQL queries, and executing them on a database. By the end, you'll have a functional assistant capable of handling real-world queries with clarity and precision.

3.5.1 Building an LLM-Powered Query Assistant
Overview of the System
The query assistant will:
1. Accept natural language inputs from a user.
2. Use an LLM to translate the input into an SQL query.
3. Validate the query against the database schema.
4. Execute the query and return the results.
5. Handle errors gracefully and provide meaningful feedback.

---

1. Setting Up the Environment
Prerequisites
- Python 3.8 or higher.
- Required libraries:
    - OpenAI for LLM interaction.
    - SQLite for the database.
    - pandas for displaying results.

Installing Required Libraries
bash

```
pip install openai pandas
```

---

2. Creating the Database
Step 1: Define the Database Schema
For this exercise, we will use a simple database sales_data.db with the following schema:

Table Name	Columns
sales_data	region, sales, year

SQL Script to Create the Database
sql

```sql
CREATE TABLE sales_data (
    region TEXT,
    sales INTEGER,
    year INTEGER
);

INSERT INTO sales_data (region, sales, year) VALUES
('North', 500000, 2023),
('South', 450000, 2023),
('East', 300000, 2023),
('West', 400000, 2023);
```

Creating the Database in Python
python

```python
import sqlite3

# Connect to SQLite database (or create it)
connection = sqlite3.connect("sales_data.db")
cursor = connection.cursor()

# Create the table and insert data
cursor.execute("""
CREATE TABLE IF NOT EXISTS sales_data (
    region TEXT,
    sales INTEGER,
    year INTEGER
);
""")
cursor.executemany("""
INSERT INTO sales_data (region, sales, year) VALUES
(?, ?, ?);
""", [
    ('North', 500000, 2023),
    ('South', 450000, 2023),
    ('East', 300000, 2023),
    ('West', 400000, 2023)
])

# Commit and close
connection.commit()
connection.close()
```

---

3. Integrating LLM for Query Translation
Step 1: OpenAI Setup
Make sure you have an OpenAI API key. Set it as an environment variable for security:
bash

```bash
export OPENAI_API_KEY="your_api_key"
```
Step 2: LLM-Powered Query Translation
python

```python
import openai

# Define the function for LLM query translation
def translate_to_sql(user_query, schema_info):
    prompt = f"""
You are a helpful assistant trained to convert
natural language into SQL queries.
Here is the database schema:
{schema_info}

Translate the following natural language query into
SQL:
'{user_query}'
"""
    response = openai.Completion.create(
        model="text-davinci-003",
        prompt=prompt,
        max_tokens=150
    )
    return response.choices[0].text.strip()
```

4. Validating and Executing SQL Queries
Step 1: Query Execution
python

```python
import sqlite3
import pandas as pd

# Function to execute the SQL query
def execute_sql_query(sql_query,
db_path="sales_data.db"):
    try:
        # Connect to the database
        connection = sqlite3.connect(db_path)
        # Execute the query and load results into a
pandas DataFrame
        df = pd.read_sql_query(sql_query, connection)
        connection.close()
        return df
```

```
    except Exception as e:
        return str(e)
```

5. Handling Errors and Clarifications
Error Feedback Loop
If an SQL error occurs, the system will provide feedback and request clarification from the LLM.
python

```
def handle_query_errors(error_message, user_query):
    clarification_prompt = f"""
The following SQL query caused an error:
Error: {error_message}

Original user query: '{user_query}'

Provide a revised query or a clarification request.
"""
    response = openai.Completion.create(
        model="text-davinci-003",
        prompt=clarification_prompt,
        max_tokens=150
    )
    return response.choices[0].text.strip()
```

6. Building the Complete Assistant
Final Script
python

```
def main():
    # Database schema
    schema_info = """
    Table: sales_data
    Columns: region (TEXT), sales (INTEGER), year
(INTEGER)
    """

    # User query
```

```python
    user_query = input("Ask a question about the
sales data: ")

    # Step 1: Translate natural language to SQL
    sql_query = translate_to_sql(user_query,
schema_info)
    print(f"\nGenerated SQL Query:\n{sql_query}")

    # Step 2: Execute the query
    result = execute_sql_query(sql_query)

    # Step 3: Handle errors
    if isinstance(result, str):  # If result is an
error message
        print(f"\nError: {result}")
        clarification = handle_query_errors(result,
user_query)
        print(f"\nLLM Suggestion:\n{clarification}")
    else:
        # Display results
        print("\nQuery Results:")
        print(result)

if __name__ == "__main__":
    main()
```

7. Testing the Query Assistant
Test 1: Simple Query
- **Input**: "Show total sales for each region."
- **Generated SQL**:

sql

```sql
SELECT region, SUM(sales) AS total_sales
FROM sales_data
GROUP BY region;
```
- **Output**:

```
  region  total_sales
0  East      300000
```

```
1  North      500000
2  South      450000
3  West       400000
```

Test 2: Ambiguous Query
- **Input**: "List top-performing regions."
- **Generated SQL**:

sql

```sql
SELECT region
FROM sales_data
WHERE sales = (SELECT MAX(sales) FROM sales_data);
```
- **Output**:

```
   region
0  North
```

Test 3: Invalid Query
- **Input**: "Find the most expensive product."
- **Generated SQL**:

sql

```sql
SELECT product, MAX(price)
FROM sales_data;
```
- **Error Handling**:

sql

```
Error: no such column: product
LLM Suggestion: Check if the 'product' column exists or rephrase the query.
```

---

8. Enhancements and Extensions

1. **Support for Multiple Tables**:
   - Add schema details for additional tables.
2. **Integration with Web Interfaces**:
   - Use frameworks like Flask or Streamlit for a user-friendly interface.
3. **Feedback Collection**:
   - Allow users to rate query results to improve prompt engineering.

This exercise demonstrated how to build a functional LLM-powered query assistant that translates natural language into SQL, executes queries, and handles errors dynamically. This tool bridges the gap between technical database management and user-friendly natural language interfaces, empowering non-technical users to interact with data effectively. With further enhancements, this assistant can evolve into a robust system for real-world applications

3.6 Key Takeaways

Query automation using Large Language Models (LLMs) is a transformative approach to accessing and analyzing data with natural language. This section summarizes the best practices for implementing reliable, efficient, and accurate query automation workflows with LLMs.

3.6.1 Best Practices for Query Automation with LLMs
1. Crafting Effective Prompts
The success of an LLM in automating queries depends heavily on the quality of prompts. A well-crafted prompt provides clarity, context, and constraints.

Key Principles for Effective Prompts
1. **Clarity**:
   - Use explicit language to minimize ambiguity.
   - Example:
     - Instead of: *"Show me the data."*
     - Use: *"List total sales for each region in 2023."*
2. **Context**:
   - Provide schema details, example queries, or explanations to guide the model.
   - Example:

plaintext

Database Schema:
Table: sales_data
Columns: region (TEXT), sales (INTEGER), year (INTEGER)

Example Query:
Input: "Show total sales by region."
Output: SELECT region, SUM(sales) AS total_sales FROM sales_data GROUP BY region;

Translate this query: "List total sales for 2023."

3. **Constraints**:
    - o Specify desired output format and SQL best practices.
    - o Example:

plaintext

Ensure the SQL includes aliases for calculated fields and uses GROUP BY for aggregations.

---

2. Validating Generated Queries

LLMs can produce incorrect or inefficient SQL queries. Always validate queries before execution.

Validation Strategies

1. **Schema Validation**:
    - o Ensure field names and table references match the database schema.
    - o Example:

python

```
def validate_schema(sql_query, schema_fields):
    missing_fields = [field for field in
sql_query.split() if field not in schema_fields]
    if missing_fields:
        return f"Invalid fields: {',
'.join(missing_fields)}"
    return "Validation passed."
```

2. **Syntax Testing**:
    - o Test the query in a sandbox environment to identify syntax errors.
    - o Example:

python

```
import sqlite3

def test_query(sql_query, db_path="sales_data.db"):
    try:
        connection = sqlite3.connect(db_path)
        connection.execute(sql_query)
        return "Query executed successfully."
    except Exception as e:
        return f"Query error: {e}"
```
3. **Output Review**:
    o Verify if the query results align with the intended user query.

---

3. Handling Ambiguity
Ambiguity in natural language inputs is a common challenge. Implement mechanisms to clarify and refine user queries.

Best Practices
1. **Follow-Up Questions**:
    o Request additional details for vague queries.
    o Example:

python

```
user_query = "Show me sales."
clarification = "Could you specify the region or time
period for the sales data?"
print(clarification)
```
2. **Error Feedback Loops**:
    o Use error messages from query execution to request refinements.
    o Example:

python

```
error_message = "Column 'region_name' does not
exist."
clarification_prompt = f"Error: {error_message}.
Could you provide more details or rephrase the
query?"
```

---

4. Optimizing Performance
Efficiency is critical for query automation systems, especially when dealing with large datasets.
Optimization Techniques
1. **Limit Data Scope**:
   - Use LIMIT clauses to restrict results for queries expected to return large datasets.
   - Example:

sql

```sql
SELECT * FROM sales_data LIMIT 100;
```

2. **Use Indexing**:
   - Ensure frequently queried fields are indexed in the database for faster execution.
3. **Batch Processing**:
   - Break down complex queries into smaller, manageable subqueries.
   - Example:

sql

```sql
WITH RegionalSales AS (
    SELECT region, SUM(sales) AS total_sales
    FROM sales_data
    GROUP BY region
)
SELECT * FROM RegionalSales WHERE total_sales > 300000;
```

---

5. Implementing Error Handling
Errors are inevitable in automated workflows. Design robust error-handling mechanisms to ensure smooth operation.

Key Components of Error Handling
1. **Error Categorization**:
   - Classify errors into syntax, logical, and data issues.
   - Example:

python

```python
def categorize_error(error_message):
    if "syntax" in error_message.lower():
        return "Syntax Error"
    elif "does not exist" in error_message.lower():
        return "Field Missing"
    else:
        return "Unknown Error"
```

2. **Automated Corrections**:
   o Use LLMs to suggest corrections or refined queries.
   o Example:

python

```python
def suggest_correction(error_message, user_query):
    prompt = f"""
    Error: {error_message}
    User Query: {user_query}
    Suggest a corrected SQL query or clarification.
    """
    response = openai.Completion.create(
        model="text-davinci-003",
        prompt=prompt,
        max_tokens=150
    )
    return response.choices[0].text.strip()
```

3. **Fallbacks**:
   o Provide users with alternatives or partial results when errors persist.

---

6. User Feedback and Iterative Improvement
Incorporate user feedback into the query automation workflow to improve accuracy and usability.

Feedback Mechanisms
1. **Rating System**:
   o Allow users to rate the quality of query results.
   o Example:

python

```python
user_rating = int(input("Rate the results (1-5): "))
```

    2. **Error Reporting**:
- Collect error reports for analysis and improvement.
- Example:

python

```python
error_report = {
    "user_query": user_query,
    "sql_query": sql_query,
    "error_message": error_message
}
```

    3. **Logs and Analytics**:
- Maintain logs of queries and outcomes for continuous monitoring.

---

7. Security and Compliance

Automating queries with LLMs must prioritize data security and compliance with regulations like GDPR or CCPA.

Best Practices

    1. **Protect Sensitive Data**:
- Avoid exposing sensitive fields in query results.
- Example:

sql

```sql
SELECT region, SUM(sales) AS total_sales
FROM sales_data
WHERE region != 'SensitiveRegion';
```

    2. **Use Environment Variables**:
- Store API keys and sensitive configurations securely.
- Example:

python

```python
import os
openai.api_key = os.getenv("OPENAI_API_KEY")
```

3. **Access Control**:
    - ○ Restrict query permissions based on user roles.

---

8. Leveraging Advanced LLM Capabilities

Modern LLMs offer features that enhance query automation.

Advanced Features

1. **Few-Shot Learning**:
    - ○ Provide examples to improve query translations.
    - ○ Example:

plaintext

```
Input: "Show total sales by region."
Output: SELECT region, SUM(sales) AS total_sales FROM sales_data
GROUP BY region;

Input: "List average sales for 2023."
Output: SELECT AVG(sales) FROM sales_data WHERE year = 2023;
```

2. **Conversational Context**:
    - ○ Maintain conversation history for multi-turn queries.
    - ○ Example:

plaintext

```
Query 1: "Show sales for 2023."
Query 2: "What about 2022?"
```

---

9. Example Workflow

Complete Code Example

python

```python
# Define schema
schema_info = """
Table: sales_data
Columns: region (TEXT), sales (INTEGER), year
(INTEGER)
"""

# User query
user_query = "Show total sales by region for 2023."
```

```
# Step 1: Translate query
sql_query = translate_to_sql(user_query, schema_info)

# Step 2: Execute query
result = execute_sql_query(sql_query)

# Step 3: Handle errors
if isinstance(result, str):
    print(f"Error: {result}")
    correction = suggest_correction(result,
user_query)
    print(f"Suggested Correction: {correction}")
else:
    print("Query Results:")
    print(result)
```

Query automation with LLMs is a powerful tool for bridging the gap between technical and non-technical users. By following best practices in prompt engineering, validation, error handling, and performance optimization, you can build robust and reliable systems that empower users to interact with data effortlessly. These guidelines ensure accuracy, efficiency, and scalability in real-world applications.

Chapter 4: Automating Data Analysis with LLMs

Automating data analysis with Large Language Models (LLMs) has the potential to revolutionize how data scientists and analysts perform routine tasks. This chapter focuses on leveraging LLMs for **Exploratory Data Analysis (EDA)**, which involves summarizing, visualizing, and interpreting data to identify patterns, trends, and anomalies.

4.1 Exploratory Data Analysis (EDA)

Exploratory Data Analysis is a critical step in understanding a dataset. It includes calculating descriptive statistics, visualizing data distributions, identifying trends, and spotting outliers. By automating EDA using LLMs, you can save time and standardize the process while maintaining analytical rigor.

4.1.1 Automating Descriptive Statistics

Descriptive statistics summarize the main characteristics of a dataset, such as the mean, median, standard deviation, and range. Automating these calculations ensures accuracy and efficiency.

1. What Are Descriptive Statistics?

Descriptive statistics provide a snapshot of the data:

- **Central Tendency**: Mean, median, mode.
- **Dispersion**: Standard deviation, variance, range.
- **Distribution Shape**: Skewness, kurtosis.

2. Automating Descriptive Statistics with Python

Example Dataset

Region	Sales	Year
North	500,000	2023
South	450,000	2023
East	300,000	2023
West	400,000	2023

Code Example: Calculating Descriptive Statistics
python

```python
import pandas as pd

# Sample dataset
data = pd.DataFrame({
    "Region": ["North", "South", "East", "West"],
    "Sales": [500000, 450000, 300000, 400000],
    "Year": [2023, 2023, 2023, 2023]
})

# Descriptive statistics
stats = data.describe()
print(stats)
```

Output:
shell

```
          Sales
count     4.000000
mean   412500.000000
std     85391.613079
min    300000.000000
25%    375000.000000
50%    425000.000000
75%    462500.000000
max    500000.000000
```

3. Using LLMs for Automating Descriptive Statistics
LLMs can automate the interpretation of descriptive statistics by providing natural language summaries.

Code Example: Generating Insights with OpenAI
python

```python
import openai

# Descriptive statistics summary
summary_prompt = """
```

```
Analyze the following dataset and provide descriptive
statistics:
Region, Sales, Year
North, 500000, 2023
South, 450000, 2023
East, 300000, 2023
West, 400000, 2023
"""

response = openai.Completion.create(
    model="text-davinci-003",
    prompt=summary_prompt,
    max_tokens=150
)

print(response.choices[0].text.strip())
```
Output:
javascript

The dataset includes sales data for four regions in 2023. The average sales are $412,500, with a maximum of $500,000 in the North region and a minimum of $300,000 in the East region. The sales distribution shows a standard deviation of $85,392, indicating moderate variability.

---

4. Key Benefits of Automation
1. **Efficiency**: Instantly generate statistical summaries.
2. **Accessibility**: Provide non-technical users with plain-language insights.
3. **Scalability**: Analyze large datasets without manual effort.

4.1.2 Identifying Trends, Outliers, and Patterns
Trends, outliers, and patterns provide deeper insights into a dataset. Automating their detection helps analysts focus on interpreting results rather than identifying anomalies manually.

---

1. Detecting Trends

Trends indicate consistent patterns over time or across categories.

Example: Visualizing Trends

python

```
import matplotlib.pyplot as plt

# Sample time-series data
sales_trend = pd.DataFrame({
    "Year": [2020, 2021, 2022, 2023],
    "Sales": [350000, 370000, 400000, 450000]
})

# Plot sales trend
plt.plot(sales_trend["Year"], sales_trend["Sales"],
marker='o')
plt.title("Sales Trend Over Time")
plt.xlabel("Year")
plt.ylabel("Sales")
plt.grid()
plt.show()
```

Output: A line chart showing a steady increase in sales over the years.

---

2. Identifying Outliers

Outliers are data points significantly different from others in the dataset.

Code Example: Detecting Outliers

python

```
# Detect outliers using the IQR method
Q1 = data["Sales"].quantile(0.25)
Q3 = data["Sales"].quantile(0.75)
IQR = Q3 - Q1

outliers = data[(data["Sales"] < (Q1 - 1.5 * IQR)) |
(data["Sales"] > (Q3 + 1.5 * IQR))]
print(outliers)
```

Output:

less

Empty DataFrame
Columns: [Region, Sales, Year]
Index: []
(No outliers detected in this dataset.)

---

3. Recognizing Patterns

Patterns reveal correlations or recurring behaviors in data.

Example: Correlation Analysis

python

```python
# Correlation between numerical columns
correlation = data.corr()
print(correlation)
```

Output:

markdown

```
        Sales
Sales   1.0
```

---

4. Automating with LLMs

LLMs can enhance pattern detection by summarizing insights and suggesting areas of focus.

Code Example: Pattern Analysis with OpenAI

python

```python
pattern_prompt = """
The dataset includes the following columns: Region,
Sales, Year.
Analyze for trends, outliers, or notable patterns in
the data:
Region, Sales, Year
North, 500000, 2023
South, 450000, 2023
East, 300000, 2023
West, 400000, 2023
"""
```

```
response = openai.Completion.create(
    model="text-davinci-003",
    prompt=pattern_prompt,
    max_tokens=150
)
```

```
print(response.choices[0].text.strip())
```
Output:
sql

The sales data shows that the North region leads in sales, while the East region has the lowest. There are no apparent outliers, and sales are moderately consistent across regions. Further analysis could explore year-over-year trends.

---

5. Visualizing Insights
Visual representations simplify the communication of trends, outliers, and patterns.
Example: Sales by Region
python

```
# Bar chart of sales by region
plt.bar(data["Region"], data["Sales"], color=['blue',
'green', 'red', 'purple'])
plt.title("Sales by Region")
plt.xlabel("Region")
plt.ylabel("Sales")
plt.show()
```
Output: A bar chart showing sales performance for each region.

---

6. Enhancing Automation
1. Combine EDA Tasks into a Workflow
Automate the entire EDA process with reusable scripts or pipelines.
Code Example: Automated EDA Workflow
python

```
def automated_eda(data):
    # Descriptive statistics
    print("Descriptive Statistics:")
```

```
    print(data.describe())

    # Detect outliers
    Q1 = data["Sales"].quantile(0.25)
    Q3 = data["Sales"].quantile(0.75)
    IQR = Q3 - Q1
    outliers = data[(data["Sales"] < (Q1 - 1.5 *
IQR)) | (data["Sales"] > (Q3 + 1.5 * IQR))]
    print("\nOutliers:")
    print(outliers if not outliers.empty else "No
outliers detected.")

    # Plot trends
    data.plot(kind='bar', x='Region', y='Sales',
title="Sales by Region")
    plt.show()

# Execute workflow
automated_eda(data)
```

By automating descriptive statistics and the detection of trends, outliers, and patterns, LLMs can significantly enhance the efficiency and accessibility of Exploratory Data Analysis. Integrating these capabilities into workflows ensures that analysts and decision-makers can focus on deriving insights and making informed decisions. The next sections will build on these fundamentals to explore deeper automation of data analysis.

4.2 Advanced Analytics

Advanced analytics builds on foundational data analysis techniques to uncover deeper insights, identify relationships, and make future predictions. In this section, we focus on two critical areas of advanced analytics: correlation and regression analysis, and time-series data forecasting using Large Language Models (LLMs).

4.2.1 Correlation and Regression Analysis

Correlation and regression analysis help quantify relationships between variables. While correlation measures the strength of association, regression predicts one variable based on another. LLMs can automate these analyses and provide interpretations.

---

1. Correlation Analysis
Definition
- Correlation quantifies the linear relationship between two variables.
- Correlation coefficient (rrr):
  - $r>0r > 0r>0$: Positive correlation.
  - $r<0r < 0r<0$: Negative correlation.
  - $r=0r = 0r=0$: No correlation.

Example Dataset
Region	Advertising Spend ($)	Sales ($)
North	10,000	50,000
South	15,000	70,000
East	20,000	90,000
West	25,000	100,000

Automating Correlation Analysis
Using Python, compute the correlation coefficient.
Code Example: Correlation Analysis
python

```
import pandas as pd

# Data
data = pd.DataFrame({
    "Advertising_Spend": [10000, 15000, 20000,
25000],
    "Sales": [50000, 70000, 90000, 100000]
})
```

```
# Correlation matrix
correlation_matrix = data.corr()
print(correlation_matrix)
```
Output:
markdown

```
            Advertising_Spend    Sales
Advertising_Spend    1.000000  0.981981
Sales                0.981981  1.000000
```

LLM-Generated Interpretation
- **Prompt**:

kotlin

The correlation coefficient between advertising spend and sales is 0.98. Interpret this result.
- **LLM Response**:

css

A correlation coefficient of 0.98 indicates a very strong positive linear relationship between advertising spend and sales. As advertising spend increases, sales tend to increase proportionally.

---

2. Regression Analysis
Definition
- Regression models predict a dependent variable based on one or more independent variables.
- **Simple Regression Equation**: $y=\beta_0+\beta_1 x+\epsilon$ $y = \beta_0 + \beta_1 x + \epsilon$ $y=\beta_0+\beta_1 x+\epsilon$
  - y: Dependent variable (e.g., Sales).
  - x: Independent variable (e.g., Advertising Spend).

Automating Regression Analysis
Code Example: Simple Linear Regression
python

```python
import statsmodels.api as sm

# Prepare data
X = data["Advertising_Spend"]
y = data["Sales"]

# Add constant for intercept
X = sm.add_constant(X)

# Build regression model
model = sm.OLS(y, X).fit()
print(model.summary())
```

Output Summary:
markdown

OLS Regression Results

==
========================

	Coef.	Std Err	t	P>|t|
Dep. Variable:	Sales R-squared:			0.964
Model:	OLS Adj. R-squared:			0.946
Coefficients:				
Intercept	30000.0	4000.0	7.5	0.01
Advertising_Spend	2.8	0.3	9.3	0.01

LLM-Generated Insights
- **Prompt**:

yaml

Based on the regression results, interpret the coefficients:
- Intercept: 30,000
- Advertising Spend Coefficient: 2.8
  - **LLM Response**:
csharp

The intercept (30,000) represents the baseline sales when advertising spend is zero. The coefficient for advertising spend (2.8) indicates that for every $1 increase in advertising spend, sales increase by $2.80.

4.2.2 Time-Series Data and Forecasting with LLMs

Time-series analysis focuses on data collected over time, such as sales trends or stock prices. LLMs can assist in automating forecasting tasks, identifying seasonal trends, and generating predictive models.

1. Time-Series Concepts
Key Components
1. **Trend**:
   - Long-term upward or downward direction in data.
2. **Seasonality**:
   - Recurring patterns over fixed periods.
3. **Noise**:
   - Random fluctuations not explained by trend or seasonality.

Example Dataset

Year	Quarter	Sales ($)
2022	Q1	50,000
2022	Q2	60,000
2022	Q3	70,000
2022	Q4	80,000
2023	Q1	55,000
2023	Q2	65,000

2. Forecasting with ARIMA
Automating ARIMA Forecasting
Code Example: ARIMA Model
python

```python
from statsmodels.tsa.arima.model import ARIMA
import pandas as pd
```

```
# Time-series data
data = pd.Series([50000, 60000, 70000, 80000, 55000,
65000],
                    index=pd.date_range(start="2022-01",
periods=6, freq="Q"))

# Fit ARIMA model
model = ARIMA(data, order=(1, 1, 1))
model_fit = model.fit()

# Forecast next 2 periods
forecast = model_fit.forecast(steps=2)
print(forecast)
```
Output:
yaml

```
2023-07-01   70500.0
2023-10-01   75500.0
Freq: Q-DEC, dtype: float64
```

LLM-Generated Interpretation
- **Prompt:**

bash

```
Based on the ARIMA forecast, sales are projected to
be $70,500 in Q3 2023 and $75,500 in Q4 2023. Explain
the trend.
```
- **LLM Response:**

css

The forecast indicates a steady increase in sales over the next two
quarters, suggesting a continued growth trend. This aligns with the
upward trajectory observed in previous data.

---

3. Seasonal Decomposition

Automating Seasonal Decomposition
Code Example: Seasonal Decompose
python

```python
from statsmodels.tsa.seasonal import
seasonal_decompose

# Decompose time-series
result = seasonal_decompose(data, model="additive",
period=4)
result.plot()
```

Generated Plot:
- **Trend**: Smooth upward movement.
- **Seasonality**: Repeats every four quarters.
- **Residuals**: Random fluctuations.

LLM-Generated Insights
- **Prompt**:
yaml

The seasonal decomposition of sales data reveals:
- Trend: Increasing over time.
- Seasonality: Peaks in Q4.
- Residuals: Minor fluctuations.
Provide actionable insights.
- **LLM Response**:
csharp

The upward trend suggests consistent growth, while the seasonality highlights Q4 as the strongest sales period. Efforts should focus on maximizing Q4 performance, with targeted marketing campaigns.

---

4. Combining LLMs with Time-Series Models

Automating Forecasting Queries

- **Prompt:**

perl

```
Forecast sales for the next two quarters using the
following historical data:
Q1 2022: $50,000, Q2 2022: $60,000, Q3 2022: $70,000,
Q4 2022: $80,000.
```

- **LLM Response:**

bash

```
Based on the historical growth rate, sales for Q1
2023 are projected at $85,000, and Q2 2023 at
$90,000.
```

Advanced analytics with LLMs enables businesses to explore relationships between variables through correlation and regression, and to predict future outcomes using time-series analysis. By automating these tasks, LLMs empower users with actionable insights, streamline workflows, and enhance data-driven decision-making. These techniques form the foundation for sophisticated analytical models covered in subsequent chapters.

4.3 Real-Time Analysis

Real-time analysis leverages live data streams to provide instant insights, enabling rapid decision-making in dynamic environments. Large Language Models (LLMs) can enhance this process by interpreting and summarizing streaming data, extracting actionable insights, and responding to queries in real time. This section covers how to integrate LLMs with streaming data systems and provides a detailed case study on real-time customer feedback analysis.

4.3.1 Integrating LLMs with Streaming Data Systems

Overview
Streaming data systems such as Apache Kafka, Apache Flink, and AWS Kinesis process data continuously as it is generated. Integrating LLMs with these systems allows for real-time analysis and decision-making by applying natural language processing (NLP) techniques to the incoming data.

---

1. Architecture for LLM Integration

Key Components
1. **Data Source**:
   - Generates real-time data (e.g., user feedback, sensor data, transaction logs).
2. **Streaming Framework**:
   - Manages data ingestion, processing, and routing.
   - Examples: Apache Kafka, Flink, AWS Kinesis.
3. **LLM Module**:
   - Processes and analyzes the data using models like GPT or BERT.
4. **Output System**:
   - Delivers insights to dashboards, alerts, or downstream systems.

Architecture Diagram
plaintext

```
Data Source → Streaming Framework → LLM Module →
Output System
```

---

2. Integrating LLMs with Apache Kafka
Step 1: Setting Up Kafka
1. **Install Kafka**:
   - Download Kafka and set up a local or cloud-based cluster.
   - Start Zookeeper and Kafka services.
2. **Define Topics**:
   - Create a topic for streaming data.

bash

```bash
kafka-topics --create --topic customer_feedback --
bootstrap-server localhost:9092 --partitions 1 --
replication-factor 1
```

Step 2: Kafka Producer for Streaming Data
Simulate real-time data using a Kafka producer.

Code Example: Kafka Producer
python

```python
from kafka import KafkaProducer
import json
import time

# Initialize Kafka producer
producer = KafkaProducer(
    bootstrap_servers='localhost:9092',
    value_serializer=lambda x:
json.dumps(x).encode('utf-8')
)

# Simulated feedback data
feedback_data = [
    {"customer_id": 1, "feedback": "Great service!",
"timestamp": "2024-01-01T12:00:00Z"},
    {"customer_id": 2, "feedback": "The product is
faulty.", "timestamp": "2024-01-01T12:01:00Z"}
]

# Send data to Kafka topic
for feedback in feedback_data:
    producer.send('customer_feedback',
value=feedback)
    time.sleep(1)  # Simulate real-time data
generation
```

Step 3: Kafka Consumer with LLM Integration

Consume data from Kafka, process it with an LLM, and generate insights.

Code Example: Kafka Consumer with OpenAI
python

```python
from kafka import KafkaConsumer
import json
import openai

# OpenAI API key
openai.api_key = "your_openai_api_key"

# Initialize Kafka consumer
consumer = KafkaConsumer(
    'customer_feedback',
    bootstrap_servers='localhost:9092',
    value_deserializer=lambda x:
json.loads(x.decode('utf-8'))
)

# Process messages with LLM
for message in consumer:
    feedback = message.value['feedback']

    # Analyze feedback with LLM
    response = openai.Completion.create(
        model="text-davinci-003",
        prompt=f"Analyze this customer feedback:
'{feedback}'",
        max_tokens=50
    )
    print(f"Feedback: {feedback}")
    print(f"Analysis:
{response.choices[0].text.strip()}")
```

3. Key Considerations

Scalability
- Use distributed processing for high data volumes.
- Optimize LLM queries by batching or fine-tuning models.

Latency
- Minimize response time by using faster models (e.g., GPT-3.5 over GPT-4 for less complex tasks).

Error Handling
- Handle data anomalies or malformed input gracefully.
- Log errors for debugging and continuous improvement.

4.3.2 Case Study: Real-Time Customer Feedback Analysis

Background

A retail company wants to analyze customer feedback in real time to address issues promptly and improve service. Feedback is collected through multiple channels (e.g., surveys, emails, and social media) and streamed into a central system for analysis.

---

1. Objectives
- Categorize feedback into predefined themes (e.g., product quality, customer service).
- Identify sentiment (positive, negative, neutral).
- Generate summaries for management dashboards.

---

2. Implementation
Step 1: Data Pipeline
1. **Data Ingestion**:
    - Use Apache Kafka to collect feedback from various sources.
2. **Real-Time Processing**:
    - Process feedback data with LLMs for categorization and sentiment analysis.
3. **Visualization**:
    - Display results on a real-time dashboard using tools like Power BI or Grafana.

Step 2: Categorizing Feedback with LLMs
Code Example: Feedback Categorization
python

```python
feedback = "The delivery was delayed, but the
customer service was helpful."

# Categorization prompt
prompt = f"""
Classify the following feedback into one of these
categories:
- Product Quality
- Delivery Service
- Customer Service
Feedback: {feedback}
"""

response = openai.Completion.create(
    model="text-davinci-003",
    prompt=prompt,
    max_tokens=50
)
print(f"Category:
{response.choices[0].text.strip()}")
```

Output:
makefile

```
Category: Delivery Service
```

Step 3: Sentiment Analysis
Code Example: Sentiment Analysis
python

```python
# Sentiment analysis prompt
prompt = f"Determine the sentiment of this feedback:
'{feedback}'. Sentiment can be Positive, Negative, or
Neutral."
```

```python
response = openai.Completion.create(
    model="text-davinci-003",
    prompt=prompt,
    max_tokens=10
)
print(f"Sentiment:
{response.choices[0].text.strip()}")
```
Output:
makefile

Sentiment: Neutral

Step 4: Real-Time Summaries
Code Example: Summarizing Feedback
python

```python
feedback_stream = [
    "The product arrived on time and works
perfectly.",
    "The customer service was unhelpful when I
reported an issue."
]

# Generate summary
summary_prompt = f"Summarize the following feedback:
{feedback_stream}"
response = openai.Completion.create(
    model="text-davinci-003",
    prompt=summary_prompt,
    max_tokens=100
)
print(f"Summary: {response.choices[0].text.strip()}")
```
Output:
sql

Summary: Most customers are satisfied with product delivery, but some
report issues with customer service responsiveness.

3. Results

- **Feedback Categorization**:
    - Product Quality: 40%
    - Delivery Service: 30%
    - Customer Service: 30%
- **Sentiment Analysis**:
    - Positive: 60%
    - Negative: 30%
    - Neutral: 10%
- **Insights**:
    - Delivery services require optimization to reduce delays.
    - Focus on improving customer service responsiveness.

4. Challenges and Solutions

Challenge	Solution
High Latency	Optimize LLM calls by batching queries or using faster models.
Data Anomalies	Implement preprocessing to clean and standardize feedback.
Scalability for High Volume	Use distributed processing and autoscaling for LLM integration.

Integrating LLMs with streaming data systems enables real-time insights, empowering organizations to respond proactively to dynamic data. The case study on customer feedback demonstrates how LLMs can enhance decision-making by automating categorization, sentiment analysis, and summarization. These techniques can be extended to various industries, including finance, healthcare, and manufacturing, for impactful real-time analytics.

4.4 Hands-On Examples

Hands-on examples provide practical applications of data analysis techniques powered by Large Language Models (LLMs). This section covers two detailed examples: automating customer churn analysis and analyzing marketing campaign performance.

4.4.1 Automating Customer Churn Analysis
Introduction

Customer churn occurs when customers stop using a product or service. Identifying and reducing churn is critical for retaining revenue and building customer loyalty. LLMs can help automate churn analysis by identifying patterns, predicting churn risks, and generating actionable insights.

Step 1: Understanding the Data
Sample Dataset

Customer ID	Monthly Charges ($)	Tenure (Months)	Churn	Support Calls
1	50	12	No	1
2	70	8	Yes	4
3	90	24	No	0
4	30	3	Yes	5

Step 2: Automating Churn Analysis
1. Exploratory Analysis

Understand key features influencing churn.

Code Example: Descriptive Statistics

python

```
import pandas as pd

# Load dataset
data = pd.DataFrame({
    "Customer ID": [1, 2, 3, 4],
    "Monthly Charges": [50, 70, 90, 30],
    "Tenure": [12, 8, 24, 3],
    "Churn": ["No", "Yes", "No", "Yes"],
    "Support Calls": [1, 4, 0, 5]
```

```
})
```

```
# Descriptive statistics
print(data.describe())
Output:
arduino
```

	Monthly Charges	Tenure	Support Calls
count	4.000000	4.000000	4.000000
mean	60.000000	11.750000	2.500000
std	25.298221	9.021493	2.380476
min	30.000000	3.000000	0.000000
max	90.000000	24.000000	5.000000

2. Identifying Correlations
Check the relationship between features and churn.
Code Example: Correlation Matrix
python

```
# Encode Churn as binary
data["Churn_Binary"] = data["Churn"].apply(lambda x:
1 if x == "Yes" else 0)

# Calculate correlations
correlation_matrix = data.corr()
print(correlation_matrix["Churn_Binary"])
```
Output:
yaml

```
Monthly Charges   -0.700
Tenure            -0.912
Support Calls      0.943
Churn_Binary       1.000
Name: Churn_Binary, dtype: float64
```

3. LLM-Powered Insights

Using OpenAI for Insights

python

```python
import openai

# Generate insights
prompt = """
Based on the following correlations with customer
churn:
- Monthly Charges: -0.70
- Tenure: -0.91
- Support Calls: 0.94

Provide actionable insights to reduce churn.
"""

response = openai.Completion.create(
    model="text-davinci-003",
    prompt=prompt,
    max_tokens=100
)
print(response.choices[0].text.strip())
```

Output:

vbnet

Customers with shorter tenures and higher support calls are more likely to churn. Focus on improving customer service quality and engagement during the early months of the customer lifecycle.

---

4. Predicting Churn

Code Example: Logistic Regression

python

```python
from sklearn.model_selection import train_test_split
from sklearn.linear_model import LogisticRegression

# Prepare data
```

```
X = data[["Monthly Charges", "Tenure", "Support
Calls"]]
y = data["Churn_Binary"]

# Train-test split
X_train, X_test, y_train, y_test =
train_test_split(X, y, test_size=0.2,
random_state=42)

# Train logistic regression model
model = LogisticRegression()
model.fit(X_train, y_train)

# Predict churn
predictions = model.predict(X_test)
print(predictions)
```

Step 3: Results
- **Key Findings**:
    - Tenure and support calls are the strongest predictors of churn.

- **Actions**:
    - Implement loyalty programs for early-stage customers.
    - Enhance customer support to address complaints promptly.

4.4.2 Analyzing Marketing Campaign Performance

Analyzing marketing campaign performance helps assess ROI, customer engagement, and overall effectiveness. LLMs can automate the evaluation of campaign results and generate strategic recommendations.

Step 1: Understanding the Data
Sample Dataset

Campaign ID	Spend ($)	Impressions	Clicks	Conversions	Revenue ($)
1	10,000	100,000	5,000	500	50,000
2	20,000	150,000	10,000	1,000	100,000
3	15,000	120,000	7,000	700	75,000

Step 2: Automating Campaign Analysis
1. Calculating Key Metrics
Code Example: ROI and Conversion Rate
python

```
# Add metrics
data["ROI"] = (data["Revenue ($)"] - data["Spend
($)"]) / data["Spend ($)"]
data["Conversion Rate"] = data["Conversions"] /
data["Clicks"]

# Display metrics
print(data[["Campaign ID", "ROI", "Conversion
Rate"]])
```
Output:

	Campaign ID	ROI	Conversion Rate
0	1	4.0	0.10
1	2	4.0	0.10
2	3	4.0	0.10

2. Identifying Trends
Code Example: Analyzing Performance
python

```
# Identify top campaign by ROI
```

```python
top_campaign = data.loc[data["ROI"].idxmax()]
print(f"Top Campaign: {top_campaign['Campaign ID']},
ROI: {top_campaign['ROI']:.2f}")
```
Output:
yaml

Top Campaign: 1, ROI: 4.00

---

3. LLM-Powered Insights
Using OpenAI to Generate Recommendations
python

```python
# Generate campaign recommendations
prompt = """
Analyze the following campaign metrics:
- Campaign 1: ROI 4.0, Conversion Rate 10%
- Campaign 2: ROI 4.0, Conversion Rate 10%
- Campaign 3: ROI 4.0, Conversion Rate 10%

Provide recommendations to optimize marketing spend
and improve campaign performance.
"""

response = openai.Completion.create(
    model="text-davinci-003",
    prompt=prompt,
    max_tokens=100
)
print(response.choices[0].text.strip())
```
Output:
vbnet

To optimize marketing spend, allocate more budget to campaigns with high ROI while exploring ways to improve conversion rates, such as targeting more qualified leads or enhancing landing page designs.

Step 3: Visualizing Results

Code Example: ROI Visualization
python

```python
import matplotlib.pyplot as plt

# Plot ROI by Campaign
plt.bar(data["Campaign ID"], data["ROI"])
plt.title("ROI by Campaign")
plt.xlabel("Campaign ID")
plt.ylabel("ROI")
plt.show()
```

Step 4: Results
- **Key Findings**:
  - All campaigns show similar ROI, indicating room for optimization in targeting and creative strategies.
- **Actions**:
  - Shift budget to the best-performing campaigns.
  - Test new targeting methods to improve conversion rates.

These hands-on examples demonstrate the power of LLMs in automating customer churn analysis and evaluating marketing campaign performance. By combining statistical techniques with LLM-generated insights, businesses can make data-driven decisions that enhance customer retention and maximize marketing ROI. These practical approaches can be applied across industries to improve operational efficiency and strategic planning.

4.5 Challenges and Troubleshooting

Automating data analysis with Large Language Models (LLMs) presents challenges, especially when handling noisy or incomplete data and optimizing performance for large datasets. This section provides detailed strategies to address these issues effectively.

4.5.1 Dealing with Noisy or Incomplete Data
1. Understanding Noisy and Incomplete Data
Noisy Data

- Data that contains errors, inconsistencies, or irrelevant information.
- **Examples**:
  - Typos in text fields (e.g., "cuustomer" instead of "customer").
  - Extreme outliers in numerical data.

Incomplete Data

- Missing values in key fields.
- **Examples**:
  - Null values for customer email addresses.
  - Missing timestamps in event logs.

---

2. Strategies for Handling Noisy Data
1. Data Cleaning
Automate data cleaning with Python libraries like pandas.
Code Example: Cleaning Typos

```python
import pandas as pd

# Sample dataset
data = pd.DataFrame({
    "Customer Name": ["Alice", "Bob", "Charl3s", "Diana"],
    "Email": ["alice@example.com", "bob@example", None, "diana@domain.com"]
})

# Correct typos using a mapping
typo_corrections = {"Charl3s": "Charles"}
data["Customer Name"] = data["Customer Name"].replace(typo_corrections)

# Fill missing emails
```

```
data["Email"] =
data["Email"].fillna("unknown@example.com")
print(data)
```
Output:
sql

	Customer Name	Email
0	Alice	alice@example.com
1	Bob	bob@example
2	Charles	unknown@example.com
3	Diana	diana@domain.com

2. Outlier Detection and Removal
Use statistical methods to identify and handle outliers.
Code Example: Removing Outliers
python

```
# Sample dataset
sales_data = pd.DataFrame({"Sales": [100, 200, 300,
10000]})

# Remove outliers using the IQR method
Q1 = sales_data["Sales"].quantile(0.25)
Q3 = sales_data["Sales"].quantile(0.75)
IQR = Q3 - Q1

# Filter out outliers
filtered_data = sales_data[(sales_data["Sales"] >=
(Q1 - 1.5 * IQR)) &
                           (sales_data["Sales"] <=
(Q3 + 1.5 * IQR))]
print(filtered_data)
```
Output:

```
   Sales
0   100
1   200
2   300
```

3. LLM-Powered Noise Reduction

Leverage LLMs to correct errors in text fields.

Code Example: Correcting Typos

python

```python
import openai

# Text with typos
text_with_typos = "The prodct delivry was delyed."

# LLM prompt for correction
prompt = f"Correct the typos in this text:
'{text_with_typos}'"
response = openai.Completion.create(
    model="text-davinci-003",
    prompt=prompt,
    max_tokens=50
)
print(response.choices[0].text.strip())
```

Output:

The product delivery was delayed.

---

3. Strategies for Handling Incomplete Data

1. Imputation Techniques

Replace missing values with appropriate substitutes.

Code Example: Imputing Missing Values

python

```python
# Fill missing values with the mean
data["Sales"] =
sales_data["Sales"].fillna(sales_data["Sales"].mean()
)
```

2. Flagging Incomplete Records

Mark rows with missing values for manual review.

Code Example: Flagging Missing Values
python

```python
data["Missing Values"] = data.isnull().any(axis=1)
print(data)
```

---

4. Best Practices for Handling Noisy or Incomplete Data
- Validate data inputs during collection.
- Use automated pipelines to clean data regularly.
- Incorporate domain knowledge into data cleaning rules.

4.5.2 Optimizing LLM Performance for Large Datasets

Challenges with Large Datasets

1. High Latency
Processing time increases with larger datasets, especially when querying LLM APIs.

2. High Costs
LLM usage costs rise with the number of API calls and tokens processed.

3. Token Limits
Many LLMs impose limits on the number of tokens per query.

Strategies to Optimize Performance

1. Preprocessing Data
Filter and preprocess data to reduce the volume of irrelevant information.

Code Example: Filtering Relevant Data
python

```python
# Filter dataset for relevant rows
filtered_data = sales_data[sales_data["Sales"] > 100]
```

```
print(filtered_data)
```

2. Batching Requests
Process large datasets in smaller batches.
Code Example: Batching API Calls
python

```python
# Batch processing for LLM API calls
batch_size = 2
for i in range(0, len(data), batch_size):
    batch = data.iloc[i:i+batch_size]
    # Send batch to LLM
    print(f"Processing batch: {batch}")
```

3. Summarization
Use LLMs to summarize data, reducing the token count.
Code Example: Summarizing a Dataset
python

```python
# Summarize data with LLM
summary_prompt = f"Summarize the following data:
{sales_data.to_dict()}"
response = openai.Completion.create(
    model="text-davinci-003",
    prompt=summary_prompt,
    max_tokens=100
)
print(response.choices[0].text.strip())
```

4. Fine-Tuning Models
Fine-tune smaller, domain-specific models for specific tasks to reduce
dependency on general-purpose LLMs.

3. Distributed Processing

Using Spark for Large Datasets
Apache Spark enables distributed processing for scalability.

Code Example: Distributed Data Processing
python

```python
from pyspark.sql import SparkSession

# Initialize Spark session
spark =
SparkSession.builder.appName("DataProcessing").getOrC
reate()

# Load large dataset
df = spark.read.csv("large_dataset.csv", header=True,
inferSchema=True)

# Perform distributed processing
filtered_df = df.filter(df["Sales"] > 100)
filtered_df.show()
```

---

4. Token Optimization

Reducing Token Usage
- Use concise prompts.
- Avoid redundant context in repeated queries.

Example: Optimized Prompt
Before:
plaintext

```
Analyze the following data:
{detailed_data}
Summarize it and highlight trends.
```

After:
plaintext

```
Summarize trends from sales data: {summary_data}
```

---

5. Best Practices for Large Dataset Analysis
- Use sampling for exploratory analysis.

- Offload preprocessing and filtering tasks to edge systems or lightweight frameworks.
- Monitor API usage and optimize configurations to minimize costs.

Handling noisy or incomplete data and optimizing LLM performance for large datasets are essential for effective data analysis. By employing robust data cleaning methods, leveraging batching and summarization, and integrating distributed processing frameworks, you can ensure that LLM-powered analysis remains efficient, scalable, and accurate. These strategies are fundamental for deploying real-world LLM systems that handle complex data challenges.

4.6 Key Takeaways

Automation Techniques and Analytical Insights
The integration of automation techniques and analytical insights through the use of Large Language Models (LLMs) has revolutionized data analysis. This section consolidates the key techniques, strategies, and insights covered in the chapter, providing a roadmap for implementing LLM-powered automation effectively.

---

1. Automation Techniques for Data Analysis
1.1 Automating Routine Analytical Tasks
LLMs simplify and accelerate routine analytical tasks by automating processes such as:
- Data cleaning
- Descriptive statistics
- Trend analysis
- Categorization and tagging
- Generating insights and summaries

Example: Automating Descriptive Statistics
python

```
import pandas as pd
```

```
# Sample data
data = pd.DataFrame({
    "Region": ["North", "South", "East", "West"],
    "Sales": [50000, 45000, 30000, 40000]
})

# Generate descriptive statistics
descriptive_stats = data["Sales"].describe()
print(descriptive_stats)
```
Output:
shell

```
count       4.000000
mean    41250.000000
std      8539.125638
min     30000.000000
25%     37500.000000
50%     42500.000000
75%     46250.000000
max     50000.000000
```

LLM-Powered Insights

How LLMs Enhance Analysis
1. **Contextual Understanding**:
   - LLMs interpret data relationships and provide nuanced insights beyond simple computation.
2. **Narrative Summaries**:
   - Generate human-readable explanations of complex data trends.

Example: LLM-Generated Summary
- **Input Prompt**:

yaml

```
Provide insights from this data:
Region: North, Sales: $50,000
```

```
Region: South, Sales: $45,000
Region: East, Sales: $30,000
Region: West, Sales: $40,000
```
- **Output**:

bash

The North region has the highest sales at $50,000, while the East region has the lowest at $30,000. Sales in the South and West regions are moderate, at $45,000 and $40,000, respectively.

1.3 Automation in Exploratory Data Analysis (EDA)

Techniques:
1. **Automating Trend Identification**:
   - Detecting and visualizing trends using Python libraries like matplotlib or seaborn.
2. **Outlier Detection**:
   - Identifying anomalies using statistical methods (e.g., Interquartile Range, Z-scores).

Code Example: Automating Outlier Detection

python

```python
# Sample data
data = pd.DataFrame({"Sales": [100, 200, 300,
10000]})

# Detect and remove outliers
Q1 = data["Sales"].quantile(0.25)
Q3 = data["Sales"].quantile(0.75)
IQR = Q3 - Q1
filtered_data = data[(data["Sales"] >= (Q1 - 1.5 *
IQR)) &
                    (data["Sales"] <= (Q3 + 1.5 *
IQR))]
print(filtered_data)
```
Output:

Sales

```
0   100
1   200
2   300
```

1.4 Advanced Analytics Techniques

Correlation and Regression
- Use correlation to quantify relationships.
- Apply regression to predict outcomes.

Code Example: Correlation Analysis
python

```python
# Correlation matrix
correlation = data.corr()
print(correlation)
```

Time-Series Forecasting
- Predict future trends with ARIMA or LSTM models.
- LLMs assist in interpreting results.

Code Example: ARIMA Forecast
python

```python
from statsmodels.tsa.arima.model import ARIMA

# Sample time-series data
sales = pd.Series([100, 200, 300, 400],
index=pd.date_range(start="2023-01-01", periods=4,
freq="M"))
model = ARIMA(sales, order=(1, 1, 1))
forecast = model.fit().forecast(steps=2)
print(forecast)
```

---

2. Analytical Insights

2.1 From Data to Actionable Insights

Transforming Data into Decisions

LLMs bridge the gap between raw data and actionable strategies by:
- Explaining trends and patterns in layman terms.
- Recommending strategies based on data insights.

Example: Marketing Campaign Analysis
- **Input**:
  - Campaign 1 ROI: 4.0
  - Campaign 2 ROI: 3.5
  - Campaign 3 ROI: 5.0
- **Output (LLM)**:

vbnet

Allocate more budget to Campaign 3, as it has the highest ROI. Consider optimizing Campaign 2 to improve its efficiency.

2.2 Real-Time Analysis and Adaptation

Real-time analysis powered by LLMs ensures instant feedback and adaptive decision-making.

Case: Customer Feedback Analysis
- Categorize feedback dynamically (e.g., Product Quality, Delivery Service).
- Generate real-time summaries for actionable insights.

Code Example: Real-Time Feedback Categorization

python

```python
# Feedback example
feedback = "The product arrived late but works well."

# LLM categorization
prompt = f"Categorize this feedback: '{feedback}'"
response = openai.Completion.create(model="text-davinci-003", prompt=prompt, max_tokens=50)
print(response.choices[0].text.strip())
```

Output:

makefile

Category: Delivery Service

2.3 Handling Challenges

Noisy or Incomplete Data
- Use LLMs for text correction and imputation.
- Automate flagging and cleaning routines.

Large Datasets
- Batch processing with LLMs for cost and efficiency.
- Use distributed frameworks (e.g., Spark) for scalability.

---

3. Best Practices for LLM-Driven Data Analysis
1. **Start with Clear Objectives**:
   - Define the problem before applying LLMs.
   - Example: "Predict churn rates" vs. "Analyze customer behavior."
2. **Use Preprocessing for Efficiency**:
   - Clean and filter data before LLM queries to optimize token usage.
3. **Leverage LLM Strengths**:
   - Use LLMs for narrative insights, summarization, and complex NLP tasks.
4. **Incorporate Human Oversight**:
   - Validate LLM-generated insights with domain experts.

Automation techniques and analytical insights powered by LLMs redefine how data analysis is performed. From simplifying routine tasks to uncovering deep insights in real time, LLMs empower users to make informed decisions quickly and effectively. By combining best practices with robust automation strategies, organizations can harness the full potential of LLM-driven analytics for competitive advantage.

Chapter 5: Data Visualization and Reporting with LLMs

Data visualization transforms raw data into meaningful insights through graphs, charts, and other visual elements. Large Language Models (LLMs) bridge the gap between natural language queries and data visualization by enabling users to generate visualizations without needing complex coding. This chapter focuses on generating visualizations using LLMs, exploring supported visualization types, and practical examples.

5.1 Natural Language to Visualization

Overview

Natural language-driven visualization allows users to describe their data analysis needs in plain English, with LLMs translating these descriptions into code for creating graphs and charts. This democratizes data visualization, making it accessible to non-technical users.

5.1.1 Generating Graphs and Charts with LLMs
1. Process Flow

1. **User Input**:
   - Natural language query specifying visualization requirements.
   - Example: *"Create a line chart of monthly sales for 2023."*
2. **LLM Translation**:
   - Converts the query into a Python script using libraries like matplotlib, seaborn, or plotly.
3. **Code Execution**:
   - The script is executed to generate the desired visualization.
4. **Output**:
   - A graph or chart displayed in a report or dashboard.

2. Hands-On Example: Creating Visualizations with LLMs
Example Dataset

Month	Sales ($)
January	50,000
February	60,000
March	55,000
April	70,000
May	65,000
June	75,000

Step 1: User Query
- Input: *"Generate a line chart showing monthly sales."*

Step 2: LLM-Generated Code

Using OpenAI for Code Generation
python

```python
import openai

# Prompt for visualization
prompt = """
Generate a Python script to create a line chart of
monthly sales using matplotlib. The dataset is:
Month: [January, February, March, April, May, June]
Sales: [50000, 60000, 55000, 70000, 65000, 75000]
"""
response = openai.Completion.create(
    model="text-davinci-003",
    prompt=prompt,
    max_tokens=150
)
print(response.choices[0].text.strip())
```

LLM Output:

python

```python
import matplotlib.pyplot as plt

# Data
months = ["January", "February", "March", "April",
"May", "June"]
sales = [50000, 60000, 55000, 70000, 65000, 75000]

# Create line chart
plt.plot(months, sales, marker='o')
plt.title("Monthly Sales")
plt.xlabel("Month")
plt.ylabel("Sales ($)")
plt.grid(True)
plt.show()
```

Step 3: Code Execution
Run the generated script to create the visualization.
Output: A line chart showing monthly sales, with months on the x-axis and sales on the y-axis.

5.1.2 Supported Visualization Types
LLMs can generate various visualization types based on the data and user query. Below are common types supported by LLMs with examples.

1. Line Graphs

Use Case:
  • Display trends over time.
Example Query:
  • Input: *"Show a line graph of daily website visitors over a week."*

Generated Code:

python

```python
import matplotlib.pyplot as plt

# Data
days = ["Monday", "Tuesday", "Wednesday", "Thursday",
"Friday", "Saturday", "Sunday"]
visitors = [120, 150, 100, 200, 250, 300, 400]

# Line chart
plt.plot(days, visitors, marker='o')
plt.title("Daily Website Visitors")
plt.xlabel("Day")
plt.ylabel("Visitors")
plt.grid(True)
plt.show()
```

2. Bar Charts

Use Case:
- Compare quantities across categories.

Example Query:
- Input: *"Create a bar chart of product sales for Q1 2023."*

Generated Code:
python

```python
import matplotlib.pyplot as plt

# Data
products = ["Product A", "Product B", "Product C"]
sales = [15000, 20000, 25000]

# Bar chart
plt.bar(products, sales, color="skyblue")
plt.title("Product Sales - Q1 2023")
plt.xlabel("Products")
plt.ylabel("Sales ($)")
plt.show()
```

3. Heatmaps

Use Case:
- Show relationships between variables in a matrix format.

Example Query:
- Input: *"Create a heatmap to display correlation between variables in a dataset."*

Generated Code:
python

```
import seaborn as sns
import pandas as pd

# Sample data
data = pd.DataFrame({
    "Variable A": [1, 2, 3, 4],
    "Variable B": [2, 3, 4, 5],
    "Variable C": [5, 6, 7, 8]
})

# Correlation matrix
correlation = data.corr()

# Heatmap
sns.heatmap(correlation, annot=True, cmap="coolwarm")
plt.title("Correlation Heatmap")
plt.show()
```

---

4. Pie Charts

Use Case:
- Show proportions of a whole.

Example Query:
- Input: *"Generate a pie chart of market share percentages."*

Generated Code:

python

```python
import matplotlib.pyplot as plt

# Data
companies = ["Company A", "Company B", "Company C"]
market_share = [40, 35, 25]

# Pie chart
plt.pie(market_share, labels=companies,
autopct='%1.1f%%', startangle=90)
plt.title("Market Share Distribution")
plt.show()
```

Best Practices for Using LLMs in Visualization
1. **Clear and Specific Queries**:
    o Provide details about the dataset and desired visualization type.
    o Example: *"Create a bar chart comparing revenue for Q1 and Q2 across three regions."*
2. **Include Dataset or Schema**:
    o Share dataset snippets or describe data fields to ensure accurate visualization.
3. **Post-Processing for Refinement**:
    o Review and refine generated code for specific formatting needs, such as labels, colors, or grid lines.
4. **Iterative Queries**:
    o If the initial visualization isn't accurate, refine the query with additional context or constraints.

Natural language to visualization is a transformative capability enabled by LLMs, simplifying data storytelling for technical and non-technical users alike. By generating Python scripts for line graphs, bar charts, heatmaps, and more, LLMs democratize the process of creating insightful visualizations, making data more accessible and actionable. These techniques are foundational for building automated reporting systems covered in the subsequent sections of this chapter.

5.2 Integrating Visualization Libraries

Integrating LLMs with popular visualization libraries such as Matplotlib, Seaborn, Plotly, and Streamlit enables seamless creation of static and interactive data visualizations. This section explores how LLM-generated commands can leverage these libraries and demonstrates automating dashboards for real-time analysis.

Using Matplotlib, Seaborn, and Plotly with LLM-Generated

Commands
1. Overview of Visualization Libraries

Library	Features
Matplotlib	Simple and versatile for static plots.
Seaborn	High-level interface for attractive statistical graphics.
Plotly	Interactive visualizations with zoom, hover, and filtering capabilities.

2. Using Matplotlib with LLM Commands
Example: Line Plot with Matplotlib
User Query: *"Generate a line plot of monthly revenue for 2023."*
Generated Code:
python

```python
import matplotlib.pyplot as plt

# Data
months = ["Jan", "Feb", "Mar", "Apr", "May", "Jun"]
revenue = [3000, 4000, 3500, 5000, 4500, 5500]

# Line plot
plt.plot(months, revenue, marker="o", linestyle="-",
color="blue")
plt.title("Monthly Revenue for 2023")
plt.xlabel("Month")
plt.ylabel("Revenue ($)")
plt.grid(True)
plt.show()
```

Output: A line plot displaying monthly revenue with markers and a grid.

---

3. Using Seaborn with LLM Commands
Example: Heatmap with Seaborn
User Query: *"Create a heatmap to show correlations in a dataset."*
Generated Code:
python

```
import seaborn as sns
import pandas as pd

# Sample data
data = pd.DataFrame({
    "Revenue": [3000, 4000, 3500, 5000],
    "Expenses": [2000, 2500, 2200, 3000],
    "Profit": [1000, 1500, 1300, 2000]
})

# Correlation matrix
correlation = data.corr()

# Heatmap
sns.heatmap(correlation, annot=True, cmap="coolwarm")
plt.title("Correlation Heatmap")
plt.show()
```
Output: A heatmap showing the correlation between Revenue, Expenses, and Profit.

---

4. Using Plotly for Interactive Visualizations
Example: Interactive Bar Chart with Plotly
User Query: *"Create an interactive bar chart for quarterly sales."*
Generated Code:
python

```
import plotly.graph_objects as go

# Data
quarters = ["Q1", "Q2", "Q3", "Q4"]
sales = [5000, 7000, 8000, 6000]
```

```python
# Interactive bar chart
fig = go.Figure(data=[
    go.Bar(name="Sales", x=quarters, y=sales,
marker_color="blue")
])
fig.update_layout(
    title="Quarterly Sales",
    xaxis_title="Quarter",
    yaxis_title="Sales ($)",
    template="plotly_dark"
)
fig.show()
```
Output: An interactive bar chart with hover functionality and zoom capabilities.

Best Practices for Using Visualization Libraries with LLMs
1. **Clearly Define the Query**:
   o Provide dataset details and specify visualization type.
   o Example: *"Create a pie chart of market shares for 2023."*
2. **Review Generated Code**:
   o Validate the syntax and customize visuals for clarity (e.g., titles, labels).
3. **Iterative Improvements**:
   o Refine visualizations based on user feedback or additional context.

5.2.2 Automating Interactive Dashboards with Streamlit

1. Overview of Streamlit
Streamlit is a Python library for building interactive dashboards and web applications quickly. It integrates seamlessly with data visualization libraries like Matplotlib, Seaborn, and Plotly.

---

2. Setting Up Streamlit
Installation
bash

```
pip install streamlit
```
Running a Streamlit Application
bash

```
streamlit run app.py
```

3. Example: Real-Time Dashboard for Sales Analysis
Step 1: Sample Dataset

Month	Sales ($)	Profit ($)
January	10,000	3,000
February	12,000	4,000
March	9,000	2,500
April	15,000	5,000

Step 2: Streamlit Dashboard Script

Code Example:
python

```python
import streamlit as st
import pandas as pd
import matplotlib.pyplot as plt

# Load data
data = pd.DataFrame({
    "Month": ["January", "February", "March",
"April"],
    "Sales": [10000, 12000, 9000, 15000],
    "Profit": [3000, 4000, 2500, 5000]
})

# Sidebar filters
st.sidebar.header("Filters")
```

```python
month_filter = st.sidebar.multiselect("Select
Months", options=data["Month"].unique(),
default=data["Month"].unique())

# Filtered data
filtered_data =
data[data["Month"].isin(month_filter)]

# Title
st.title("Sales and Profit Dashboard")

# Line Chart
st.subheader("Sales Over Time")
plt.figure(figsize=(8, 4))
plt.plot(filtered_data["Month"],
filtered_data["Sales"], marker="o", label="Sales")
plt.plot(filtered_data["Month"],
filtered_data["Profit"], marker="o", label="Profit",
linestyle="--")
plt.legend()
plt.xlabel("Month")
plt.ylabel("Amount ($)")
plt.title("Monthly Sales and Profit")
st.pyplot(plt)

# Data Table
st.subheader("Filtered Data")
st.dataframe(filtered_data)
```

4. Key Features of the Dashboard
1. **Interactive Filters**:
    - Users can select specific months to visualize.
2. **Dynamic Updates**:
    - Visualizations and data tables update in real time based on user inputs.
3. **Multiple Visualizations**:
    - Include line charts, bar charts, and data tables for comprehensive analysis.

5. Expanding the Dashboard
Adding Plotly Visualizations

Enhance interactivity by integrating Plotly.

Code Example:

python

```
import plotly.express as px

# Plotly Bar Chart
fig = px.bar(filtered_data, x="Month", y="Sales",
title="Sales by Month")
st.plotly_chart(fig)
```

Connecting Live Data

Connect to streaming data sources (e.g., Kafka, databases) for real-time updates.

Code Example:

python

```
import time

# Simulate live updates
for i in range(10):
    st.write(f"Live update {i+1}")
    time.sleep(1)
```

---

6. Best Practices for Streamlit Dashboards
1. **Keep Interfaces Intuitive**:
   - Use clear labels and tooltips for better user experience.
2. **Ensure Scalability**:
   - Optimize code for large datasets by using caching and efficient data queries.
3. **Integrate Multiple Data Sources**:
   - Combine databases, APIs, and static files for a holistic view.
4. **Iterate Based on User Feedback**:

- o Continuously improve the dashboard based on usage insights.

Integrating LLMs with visualization libraries like Matplotlib, Seaborn, and Plotly simplifies the process of creating data visualizations. Automating interactive dashboards with Streamlit elevates these visualizations into actionable tools for real-time decision-making. Together, these technologies empower both technical and non-technical users to derive insights, making data visualization accessible, engaging, and effective.

5.3 Dynamic Reporting

Dynamic reporting combines data visualization with automated summaries to provide actionable insights. By leveraging LLMs, organizations can create reports that integrate visual elements and concise summaries, significantly enhancing decision-making processes. This section explores automating report summaries and generating use-case-specific dashboards like weekly sales dashboards.

5.3.1 Automating Report Summaries with Visual Insights
1. The Importance of Report Summaries
Automated summaries add narrative context to visual insights, making reports more interpretable. Summaries generated by LLMs highlight key patterns, trends, and actionable recommendations directly from the data.

2. Steps to Automate Report Summaries
Step 1: Data Preparation
Ensure that the dataset is cleaned, structured, and ready for analysis.

Example Dataset

Region	Sales ($)	Profit ($)	Year
North	50,000	15,000	2023
South	40,000	12,000	2023
East	60,000	18,000	2023
West	55,000	16,000	2023

Step 2: Visualizing Data

Create a visualization to complement the summary.

Code Example: Bar Chart for Regional Sales

python

```python
import matplotlib.pyplot as plt

# Data
regions = ["North", "South", "East", "West"]
sales = [50000, 40000, 60000, 55000]

# Bar Chart
plt.bar(regions, sales, color="skyblue")
plt.title("Regional Sales - 2023")
plt.xlabel("Region")
plt.ylabel("Sales ($)")
plt.show()
```

Output: A bar chart displaying sales performance across regions.

Step 3: LLM-Generated Summary

Integrate an LLM to generate a narrative summary from the dataset.

Using OpenAI for Summaries

python

```python
import openai

# Prompt for summary
prompt = """
Analyze the following data:
Region: [North: 50000, South: 40000, East: 60000,
West: 55000]
Provide a summary highlighting top-performing regions
and actionable insights.
"""

response = openai.Completion.create(
    model="text-davinci-003",
    prompt=prompt,
    max_tokens=100
```

```
)
print(response.choices[0].text.strip())
```

Output:
bash

The East region recorded the highest sales at $60,000, followed by the West at $55,000. The South region had the lowest sales at $40,000. Consider allocating more resources to the South region to boost performance.

---

3. Automating Comprehensive Reports
Combine visualizations and summaries into a single report.
Code Example: Dynamic Report
python

```python
# Generate Report
def generate_report():
    # Visualization
    plt.bar(regions, sales, color="skyblue")
    plt.title("Regional Sales - 2023")
    plt.xlabel("Region")
    plt.ylabel("Sales ($)")
    plt.savefig("regional_sales_chart.png")
    plt.close()

    # LLM Summary
    response = openai.Completion.create(
        model="text-davinci-003",
        prompt="Analyze sales data and provide a
summary.",
        max_tokens=100
    )
    summary = response.choices[0].text.strip()

    # Create Report
    with open("sales_report.txt", "w") as report:
        report.write("**Sales Report 2023**\n\n")
        report.write("Summary:\n")
```

```
        report.write(summary + "\n\n")
        report.write("Visualization saved as
'regional_sales_chart.png'.\n")

generate_report()
```

---

4. Benefits of Automated Report Summaries
- **Speed**: Generate insights instantly from large datasets.
- **Clarity**: Combine data visuals with narratives for easy comprehension.
- **Actionability**: Highlight recommendations directly from trends and anomalies.

5.3.2 Use Case: Generating Weekly Sales Dashboards
1. Purpose of Weekly Sales Dashboards
Weekly dashboards track sales performance, identify short-term trends, and enable timely decisions. Automating this process ensures consistency and reduces manual effort.

---

2. Workflow for Weekly Dashboards
Step 1: Define the Data
Collect and structure weekly sales data.
Example Dataset

Week	Sales ($)	Profit ($)
Week 1	10,000	3,000
Week 2	12,000	4,000
Week 3	9,000	2,500
Week 4	15,000	5,000

Step 2: Create a Visualization
Code Example: Line Chart for Weekly Sales
python

```
# Data
weeks = ["Week 1", "Week 2", "Week 3", "Week 4"]
sales = [10000, 12000, 9000, 15000]
```

```python
# Line Chart
plt.plot(weeks, sales, marker="o", linestyle="--",
color="green")
plt.title("Weekly Sales - January 2023")
plt.xlabel("Week")
plt.ylabel("Sales ($)")
plt.grid(True)
plt.show()
```
Output: A line chart showing weekly sales trends.

Step 3: Generate Insights
Using LLMs for Insights
python

```python
# Weekly sales summary
prompt = """
Weekly sales data: Week 1: $10,000, Week 2: $12,000,
Week 3: $9,000, Week 4: $15,000
Summarize the trends and provide actionable
recommendations.
"""

response = openai.Completion.create(
    model="text-davinci-003",
    prompt=prompt,
    max_tokens=100
)
print(response.choices[0].text.strip())
```
Output:
vbnet

Sales peaked in Week 4 at $15,000, while Week 3 recorded the lowest at $9,000. Focus on strategies to sustain high sales during Week 4 and address factors contributing to the dip in Week 3.

Step 4: Automate Dashboard Generation
Create a reusable script to automate weekly dashboards.
Code Example: Automating Dashboards with Streamlit

python

```python
import streamlit as st

# Load Data
data = {
    "Week": ["Week 1", "Week 2", "Week 3", "Week 4"],
    "Sales": [10000, 12000, 9000, 15000],
    "Profit": [3000, 4000, 2500, 5000]
}

# Sidebar Filter
st.sidebar.title("Weekly Sales Dashboard")
selected_week = st.sidebar.selectbox("Select Week",
data["Week"])

# Display Data
st.title("Weekly Sales Performance")
st.line_chart(data={"Sales": data["Sales"]})

# Generate Insights
st.subheader("Insights")
if selected_week == "Week 4":
    st.write("Sales peaked in Week 4. Focus on
maintaining this trend.")
elif selected_week == "Week 3":
    st.write("Sales dropped in Week 3. Investigate
contributing factors.")
else:
    st.write("Performance was stable.")
```

3. Key Features of Weekly Dashboards
1. **Real-Time Updates**:
   - Connect to live sales databases for dynamic updates.
2. **Interactive Filters**:
   - Allow users to drill down into specific weeks or products.
3. **Visual and Narrative Insights**:
   - Combine line charts with LLM-generated summaries.

Dynamic reporting with automated summaries and visual insights transforms raw data into actionable knowledge. By automating weekly sales dashboards, organizations can monitor performance, identify trends, and make informed decisions in real time. LLMs empower users by simplifying complex data analysis and generating narrative insights, creating a seamless bridge between data and decision-making.

5.4 Challenges and Optimization

Creating effective visualizations with Large Language Models (LLMs) requires addressing challenges such as ensuring accuracy in visual representations and handling large datasets. This section explores these challenges and provides actionable strategies for optimization.

5.4.1 Ensuring Accuracy in Visual Representations
1. Importance of Accuracy in Visualizations
Accurate visualizations are critical for:
- Representing data truthfully.
- Enabling effective decision-making.
- Avoiding misinterpretation of trends or patterns.

2. Common Challenges in Ensuring Accuracy
1. Misalignment Between Data and Visuals
- Occurs when incorrect data points are plotted or when axes are mislabeled.

Example Issue: A bar chart showing sales may incorrectly label the x-axis as "Regions" instead of "Products."

2. Overcomplication
- Overloading visuals with too many elements, such as excessive labels, colors, or data points, leading to confusion.

3. Scaling and Proportion Errors
- Distorting proportions on axes can misrepresent data trends.

Example Issue: An inconsistent y-axis scale exaggerates differences between data points.

---

3. Strategies for Ensuring Accuracy
1. Validation of Data

- Double-check the dataset before visualization.
- Automate validation with Python.

Code Example: Data Validation

python

```
import pandas as pd

# Sample dataset
data = pd.DataFrame({
    "Region": ["North", "South", "East", "West"],
    "Sales": [50000, 40000, 60000, 55000]
})

# Validate for missing or inconsistent data
if data.isnull().values.any():
    print("Dataset contains missing values.")
else:
    print("Dataset is clean.")
```

---

2. Automating Labeling and Scaling
Ensure labels and scales are dynamically generated based on the data.
Code Example: Dynamic Labeling
python

```
import matplotlib.pyplot as plt

# Data
regions = ["North", "South", "East", "West"]
sales = [50000, 40000, 60000, 55000]

# Bar Chart
plt.bar(regions, sales, color="skyblue")
plt.title("Regional Sales - 2023")
plt.xlabel("Region")
```

```
plt.ylabel("Sales ($)")
plt.ylim(0, max(sales) + 10000)  # Dynamic scaling
plt.show()
```

3. LLM-Assisted Validation

Use LLMs to verify that the visualization matches the dataset.
Example:
- Prompt: *"Verify if the following chart accurately represents the dataset: Sales by region: North: 50,000, South: 40,000, East: 60,000, West: 55,000."*
- LLM Output: *"The chart correctly represents the data with accurate labels and scaling."*

4. Common Practices for Visual Accuracy
1. **Use Consistent Scales**:
   - Maintain proportional scales on axes to avoid distortion.
2. **Keep Visuals Simple**:
   - Limit the number of data points and avoid clutter.
3. **Add Annotations**:
   - Highlight key points to improve interpretability.

5.4.2 Handling Large Datasets for Visualization
1. Challenges of Visualizing Large Datasets
1. Overcrowded Visuals
- Displaying too many data points can make charts unreadable.
2. Performance Bottlenecks
- Processing and rendering large datasets can slow down systems.
3. Aggregation and Sampling
- Aggregated data may miss fine details, while sampled data might overlook key patterns.

2. Strategies for Handling Large Datasets
1. Data Sampling
- Use representative samples to reduce dataset size while preserving key trends.
Code Example: Random Sampling

python

```python
# Sample 10% of the dataset
sampled_data = data.sample(frac=0.1, random_state=42)
print(sampled_data)
```

2. Aggregation
- Group data into meaningful categories to simplify visualization.

Code Example: Aggregating Data

python

```python
# Group sales by region
aggregated_data =
data.groupby("Region")["Sales"].sum()
print(aggregated_data)
```

3. Incremental Visualization
- Break data into smaller chunks and visualize them incrementally.

Code Example: Incremental Visualization

python

```python
for chunk in pd.read_csv("large_dataset.csv",
chunksize=1000):
    chunk.plot(kind="line", x="Date", y="Sales")
    plt.show()
```

4. Using High-Performance Libraries
- Libraries like Plotly, Bokeh, or Dash handle large datasets efficiently with interactive capabilities.

Code Example: Interactive Plot with Plotly

python

```python
import plotly.express as px

# Data
large_data = pd.DataFrame({
    "Date": pd.date_range(start="2023-01-01",
periods=1000, freq="D"),
```

```
    "Sales": pd.np.random.randint(100, 1000,
size=1000)
})

# Plot
fig = px.line(large_data, x="Date", y="Sales",
title="Sales Over Time")
fig.show()
```

3. Optimizing Visualization for Performance
1. Preprocessing Data
- Remove unnecessary columns and rows before visualization.

Code Example: Data Filtering
python

```
filtered_data = data[data["Sales"] > 1000]
```

2. Caching Results
- Cache processed data to avoid redundant computations.

Using Streamlit Caching
python

```
import streamlit as st

@st.cache
def load_data():
    return pd.read_csv("large_dataset.csv")
data = load_data()
```

3. Asynchronous Loading
- Load and render data asynchronously to improve user experience in dashboards.

4. Comparing Visualization Libraries for Large Datasets

Library	Advantages	Use Case
Matplotlib	Simple, static plots.	Small datasets and quick

Library	Advantages	Use Case
		visuals.
Seaborn	Attractive statistical plots.	Aggregated datasets.
Plotly	Interactive and scalable.	Large datasets with interactivity.
Bokeh	Web-ready, high-performance plots.	Real-time web applications.

Ensuring accuracy and optimizing performance are critical for effective visualizations. By validating data, simplifying visuals, and leveraging efficient libraries, LLMs can transform even large datasets into clear, actionable insights. These strategies are essential for creating reliable, scalable, and impactful visualizations in real-world applications.

5.5 Interactive Exercise: Building a Data Dashboard Using LLMs

Dashboards are powerful tools for visualizing data and providing actionable insights in real time. Building a data dashboard using Large Language Models (LLMs) streamlines the process by automating the creation of visualizations and summaries. This interactive exercise walks through building a fully functional data dashboard using Python, Streamlit, and LLM-powered automation.

5.5.1 Building a Data Dashboard Using LLMs
Objective
To build an interactive data dashboard that:
1. Visualizes data dynamically.
2. Generates automated insights using LLMs.
3. Updates in real time based on user input.

Step 1: Define the Dataset
Sample Dataset

Month	Region	Sales ($)	Profit ($)
January	North	50,000	15,000
February	South	40,000	12,000
March	East	60,000	18,000
April	West	55,000	16,000

Save the dataset as sales_data.csv.

Step 2: Install Required Libraries
Install the following libraries:
bash

```
pip install streamlit pandas matplotlib openai
```

Step 3: Set Up OpenAI API
1. Obtain your OpenAI API key from OpenAI.
2. Add the key to your environment:

bash

```
export OPENAI_API_KEY="your_api_key"
```

Step 4: Dashboard Code
Code Example
Save the following script as data_dashboard.py:
python

```python
import streamlit as st
import pandas as pd
import matplotlib.pyplot as plt
import openai

# Set OpenAI API key
openai.api_key = "your_api_key"

# Load Dataset
@st.cache
def load_data():
    return pd.read_csv("sales_data.csv")
```

```python
data = load_data()

# Sidebar Filters
st.sidebar.title("Filters")
selected_month = st.sidebar.multiselect("Select
Month", options=data["Month"].unique(),
default=data["Month"].unique())
selected_region = st.sidebar.multiselect("Select
Region", options=data["Region"].unique(),
default=data["Region"].unique())

# Filter Data
filtered_data =
data[(data["Month"].isin(selected_month)) &
(data["Region"].isin(selected_region))]

# Dashboard Title
st.title("Interactive Sales Dashboard")

# Display Filtered Data
st.subheader("Filtered Data")
st.dataframe(filtered_data)

# Visualization: Bar Chart for Sales
st.subheader("Sales by Region")
fig, ax = plt.subplots()
filtered_data.groupby("Region")["Sales
($)"].sum().plot(kind="bar", ax=ax, color="skyblue")
ax.set_title("Total Sales by Region")
ax.set_xlabel("Region")
ax.set_ylabel("Sales ($)")
st.pyplot(fig)

# Visualization: Line Chart for Monthly Trends
st.subheader("Monthly Sales Trend")
fig, ax = plt.subplots()
filtered_data.groupby("Month")["Sales
($)"].sum().plot(kind="line", ax=ax, marker="o",
color="green")
```

```python
ax.set_title("Monthly Sales Trend")
ax.set_xlabel("Month")
ax.set_ylabel("Sales ($)")
st.pyplot(fig)

# LLM Insights
st.subheader("Automated Insights")
insight_prompt = f"""
Analyze the following filtered sales data:
{filtered_data.to_dict(orient='records')}
Provide key trends and recommendations.
"""
response = openai.Completion.create(
    model="text-davinci-003",
    prompt=insight_prompt,
    max_tokens=150
)
st.write(response.choices[0].text.strip())
```

Step 5: Run the Dashboard
Run the script using Streamlit:
bash

```
streamlit run data_dashboard.py
```

Step 6: Interacting with the Dashboard
1. **Data Filters**:
   - Use the sidebar to filter data by month and region.
   - The dashboard dynamically updates based on your selections.
2. **Visualizations**:
   - **Bar Chart**:
     - Shows total sales for each region.
   - **Line Chart**:
     - Displays monthly sales trends.
3. **Automated Insights**:
   - LLM generates insights based on filtered data.
   - Example Output:

vbnet

The East region has the highest sales at $60,000. January and February have lower sales compared to March and April. Focus on boosting sales in the North and South regions.

Customization Options
Add More Visualizations
- **Profit by Region**:

python

```
fig, ax = plt.subplots()
filtered_data.groupby("Region")["Profit
($)"].sum().plot(kind="bar", ax=ax,
color="lightcoral")
ax.set_title("Total Profit by Region")
ax.set_xlabel("Region")
ax.set_ylabel("Profit ($)")
st.pyplot(fig)
```

Connect to a Live Data Source
- Replace the static CSV file with a live database connection (e.g., MySQL, PostgreSQL, or Google Sheets).

Enhance LLM Prompts
- Add context or specific questions to the prompts to generate actionable recommendations.

Step 7: Best Practices
1. **Ensure Data Accuracy**:
    - Validate data before loading into the dashboard.
2. **Optimize Performance**:
    - Use caching (@st.cache) to speed up loading times for large datasets.
3. **Design Intuitive Layouts**:
    - Arrange filters, charts, and insights logically for ease of use.
4. **Iterate with Feedback**:
    - Improve the dashboard based on user testing and feedback.

This exercise demonstrates the power of LLMs in building interactive, data-driven dashboards. By combining visualization tools like Matplotlib with Streamlit's interactivity and OpenAI's insights, you can create dashboards that are both functional and user-friendly. This approach is scalable across industries, from sales analysis to healthcare and finance, making it an invaluable skill for modern data professionals.

5.6 Key Takeaways

5.6.1 Best Practices for Visualization and Reporting
Effective data visualization and reporting are crucial for interpreting complex datasets and making informed decisions. This section highlights best practices to ensure clarity, accuracy, and actionability in visualizations and reporting.

---

1. Principles of Effective Data Visualization
1.1 Clarity and Simplicity
- Visualizations should present information clearly, avoiding clutter and overcomplication.
- **Key Actions**:
    - Use appropriate chart types (e.g., bar charts for comparisons, line charts for trends).
    - Limit the number of colors, labels, and data points.

Example: Simple Bar Chart

python

```
import matplotlib.pyplot as plt

# Data
regions = ["North", "South", "East", "West"]
sales = [50000, 40000, 60000, 55000]

# Bar chart
plt.bar(regions, sales, color="skyblue")
plt.title("Regional Sales - 2023")
plt.xlabel("Region")
plt.ylabel("Sales ($)")
```

```
plt.show()
```

Output: A clean bar chart that focuses on the key comparison of regional sales.

1.2 Accuracy in Representations

- Ensure visualizations represent the data truthfully without distortion.
- **Key Actions**:
    - o Maintain consistent scaling across axes.
    - o Verify that labels, legends, and annotations match the data.

Example of Accurate Scaling

python

```
plt.bar(regions, sales, color="skyblue")
plt.ylim(0, max(sales) + 10000)   # Set y-axis to
accommodate data range
plt.show()
```

1.3 Context and Relevance

- Provide context to help viewers understand the data.
- **Key Actions**:
    - o Add titles, axis labels, and legends.
    - o Use annotations to highlight key points.

Example: Annotating a Chart

python

```
for i, value in enumerate(sales):
    plt.text(i, value + 1000, f"${value}",
ha="center")
```

---

2. Best Practices for Reporting

2.1 Automate Reporting Processes

Automate repetitive tasks in reporting to save time and ensure consistency.

Example: Automated Summary

Code Example:

python

```python
import openai

# Dataset summary
data_summary = """
Region: North, Sales: 50000
Region: South, Sales: 40000
Region: East, Sales: 60000
Region: West, Sales: 55000
"""

# Generate automated insights
response = openai.Completion.create(
    model="text-davinci-003",
    prompt=f"Summarize the following sales
data:\n{data_summary}",
    max_tokens=100
)
print(response.choices[0].text.strip())
```
Output:
bash

The East region leads in sales with $60,000, followed by the West at $55,000. Focus on improving performance in the South region, which has the lowest sales at $40,000.

2.2 Incorporate Visual and Narrative Insights
Combine charts and text to enhance understanding.
Example: Combining Visuals and Text
1. Create a bar chart to compare regional sales.
2. Use LLMs to generate a summary explaining the chart.

2.3 Make Reports Interactive
Interactive dashboards allow users to explore data dynamically.
Example: Streamlit Dashboard

python

```python
import streamlit as st
```

```python
import pandas as pd

# Sample data
data = pd.DataFrame({
    "Region": ["North", "South", "East", "West"],
    "Sales": [50000, 40000, 60000, 55000]
})

# Sidebar filter
selected_region = st.sidebar.selectbox("Select
Region", data["Region"].unique())

# Filtered data
filtered_data = data[data["Region"] ==
selected_region]

# Display data
st.title("Regional Sales Report")
st.bar_chart(filtered_data)
```

2.4 Ensure Accessibility
- Use accessible color schemes and ensure charts are readable for all viewers.
- **Key Actions**:
    - Choose colorblind-friendly palettes.
    - Add text descriptions for visual elements.

---

3. Advanced Techniques for Optimization
3.1 Handling Large Datasets
Optimize visualization for large datasets to prevent performance bottlenecks.
Key Techniques:
- Aggregate data to focus on high-level trends.
- Use libraries like Plotly or Bokeh for efficient rendering.

3.2 Automate Dashboards with Live Data
Connect dashboards to real-time data sources for up-to-date insights.
Code Example: Connecting to a Database

python

```python
import sqlalchemy

# Connect to SQL database
engine =
sqlalchemy.create_engine("sqlite:///sales.db")
data = pd.read_sql("SELECT * FROM sales", engine)
```

4. Common Challenges and Solutions

Challenge	Solution
Overcrowded Visualizations	Simplify by focusing on key data points and aggregating details.
Inconsistent Axes	Use dynamic scaling to ensure accurate representation of data.
Performance Bottlenecks	Optimize queries and use high-performance visualization libraries.
User Misinterpretation	Add annotations and narrative summaries to clarify visualizations.

5. Best Practices Checklist

Aspect	Best Practice
Clarity	Use simple, focused visuals with clear labels and legends.
Accuracy	Validate data before visualization and avoid scaling distortions.
Context	Add titles, annotations, and legends to provide meaningful context.
Interactivity	Enable user exploration through filters and interactive charts.
Automation	Automate reporting to save time and maintain consistency.
Optimization	Aggregate large datasets and use efficient libraries for performance.

Best practices for visualization and reporting focus on clarity, accuracy, and relevance, ensuring that data is presented in a way that drives informed decision-making. By integrating LLMs, automating workflows, and optimizing processes, you can create impactful reports that combine visual and narrative insights to empower users. These principles lay a strong foundation for advanced data storytelling and dynamic reporting in real-world scenarios.

Chapter 6: Decision-Making with Data LLMs

In today's data-driven world, the ability to extract actionable insights from data is crucial for effective decision-making. Large Language Models (LLMs) take this a step further by transforming raw analysis into comprehensible insights and decision support systems that can guide organizational strategy and operations. This chapter explores how to turn analytical insights into decision-support systems and explains how to present insights in a human-friendly manner.

6.1 From Insights to Actions

The journey from raw data to actionable decisions involves processing, analyzing, interpreting, and presenting the data in ways that stakeholders can act upon. LLMs simplify this process by automating analysis, generating recommendations, and presenting insights in plain language.

6.1.1 Turning Analysis into Decision Support Systems

A **Decision Support System (DSS)** is a computer-based application that helps organizations make informed decisions by integrating data analysis, visualization, and actionable recommendations. With LLMs, you can automate key elements of these systems.

1. Elements of an LLM-Powered Decision Support System
1.1 Data Input
- Ingest structured and unstructured data from multiple sources.
- Examples: Databases, APIs, spreadsheets, and real-time sensors.

1.2 Data Analysis
- Use statistical models, machine learning, or LLMs for processing and analyzing data.
- Example: Forecast sales trends, identify customer churn risks, or detect anomalies.

1.3 Insight Generation

- Generate actionable insights based on analysis.
- Example: "Sales are expected to increase by 15% next quarter due to seasonal demand."

1.4 Recommendations
- Provide actionable next steps based on insights.
- Example: "Increase inventory levels for Product A by 20% to meet projected demand."

---

2. Building a Simple DSS
Example Use Case: Inventory Management
Scenario: A retail store wants to optimize inventory levels based on sales trends.

Step 1: Input Data

Product	Current Stock	Monthly Sales	Lead Time (Days)
Product A	50	30	7
Product B	100	20	10
Product C	200	50	15

Step 2: Analyze Data
Analyze sales trends to forecast future demand.
Code Example: Forecasting Demand
python

```python
import pandas as pd

# Load data
data = pd.DataFrame({
    "Product": ["Product A", "Product B", "Product
C"],
    "Current Stock": [50, 100, 200],
    "Monthly Sales": [30, 20, 50],
    "Lead Time (Days)": [7, 10, 15]
})

# Calculate reorder levels
data["Reorder Level"] = (data["Monthly Sales"] / 30)
* data["Lead Time (Days)"]
```

```
data["Reorder Needed"] = data["Current Stock"] <
data["Reorder Level"]

print(data)
```
Output:

Product	Current Stock	Reorder Level	Reorder Needed
Product A	50	7	False
Product B	100	6.67	False
Product C	200	25	False

Step 3: Generate Insights
Use LLMs to provide human-readable insights.
LLM Example: Input Prompt:
plaintext

Based on the following inventory data:
- Product A: Current Stock = 50, Reorder Level = 7
- Product B: Current Stock = 100, Reorder Level = 6.67
- Product C: Current Stock = 200, Reorder Level = 25
Explain if reorders are needed.

LLM Output:
plaintext

No reorders are needed at this time. All products have sufficient stock to meet projected demand.

Step 4: Add Recommendations
Example Recommendations:
- Monitor Product C's stock closely as demand is higher relative to others.
- Re-evaluate reorder levels weekly to account for fluctuating sales.

3. Integrating DSS into Real-Time Dashboards
Streamlit Example:
python

```python
import streamlit as st

# Display data
st.title("Inventory Management Dashboard")
st.dataframe(data)

# Highlight reorder recommendations
for _, row in data.iterrows():
    if row["Reorder Needed"]:
        st.write(f"Reorder {row['Product']}
immediately.")
    else:
        st.write(f"{row['Product']} has sufficient
stock.")
```

Benefits of LLM-Powered DSS
1. **Speed**: Automates analysis and insight generation.
2. **Scalability**: Handles large datasets and integrates multiple data sources.
3. **Actionability**: Provides clear recommendations for stakeholders.

6.1.2 Explaining Insights in Human-Friendly Language
1. Importance of Human-Friendly Explanations
Insights need to be comprehensible to all stakeholders, including those without technical expertise. LLMs excel at translating complex data into plain language.

2. Techniques for Human-Friendly Explanations
1. Simplify Jargon
Avoid technical terms or explain them in simple language.
Example:
- **Before**: "The correlation coefficient is 0.9, indicating a strong positive relationship."
- **After**: "Sales and advertising spend are strongly linked; higher advertising often leads to increased sales."

2. Focus on Actionable Outcomes
Present insights that lead to clear actions.

Example:
- Insight: "Customer churn rates are rising in Q4."
- Recommendation: "Introduce loyalty discounts and personalized offers to retain customers."

3. Use Examples and Visuals
Combine narrative insights with charts or examples to reinforce understanding.
Example: **Insight:** "East region sales grew by 20%, while West region sales dropped by 10%." **Visualization:** Bar chart comparing regional sales performance.

3. Using LLMs to Explain Insights
Scenario: Monthly Sales Analysis
Data:

Month	Sales ($)
Jan	50,000
Feb	45,000
Mar	55,000

LLM Prompt:
plaintext

Analyze the monthly sales data: January: $50,000, February: $45,000, March: $55,000. Provide insights and recommendations.

LLM Response:
plaintext

Sales dipped slightly in February but recovered in March, showing a 22% increase. Focus on maintaining the momentum by promoting high-performing products.

4. Best Practices for Explaining Insights

Aspect	Best Practice
Clarity	Use plain language to explain technical terms.

Aspect	Best Practice
Actionability	Highlight specific actions based on insights.
Visual Support	Complement insights with charts, graphs, or tables.
Contextualization	Relate findings to business goals or operational challenges.

The ability to turn data into actionable insights is a cornerstone of effective decision-making. By leveraging LLMs, organizations can streamline this process, making insights accessible to all stakeholders and integrating them into decision-support systems. Whether it's inventory management, sales analysis, or customer retention, the combination of automated analysis and human-friendly explanations ensures clarity, relevance, and impact.

6.2 What-If and Scenario Analysis

What-if and scenario analysis are critical tools in decision-making, allowing businesses to evaluate potential outcomes and risks based on historical data and simulated conditions. LLMs enhance these processes by automating predictions, simulating business scenarios, and presenting actionable insights in a comprehensible format.

6.2.1 Predicting Outcomes Using Historical Data
1. Overview
Historical data provides a foundation for forecasting future outcomes. By identifying trends, patterns, and correlations, businesses can predict variables like sales, revenue, and customer behavior. LLMs streamline this process by generating predictions based on historical inputs and presenting insights in actionable language.

2. Steps to Predict Outcomes
Step 1: Data Preparation
Historical data must be cleaned, structured, and validated before analysis.
Example Dataset

Year	Month	Sales ($)
2022	Jan	50,000

Year	Month	Sales ($)
2022	Feb	52,000
2022	Mar	48,000
2023	Jan	55,000
2023	Feb	57,000

Step 2: Trend Analysis

Use statistical techniques or LLMs to identify patterns in the data.

Code Example: Sales Trend Analysis

python

```python
import pandas as pd
import matplotlib.pyplot as plt

# Data
data = pd.DataFrame({
    "Year": [2022, 2022, 2022, 2023, 2023],
    "Month": ["Jan", "Feb", "Mar", "Jan", "Feb"],
    "Sales": [50000, 52000, 48000, 55000, 57000]
})

# Plot sales trend
plt.plot(data["Month"][:3], data["Sales"][:3],
label="2022", marker="o")
plt.plot(data["Month"][3:], data["Sales"][3:],
label="2023", marker="o")
plt.title("Sales Trend Comparison")
plt.xlabel("Month")
plt.ylabel("Sales ($)")
plt.legend()
plt.show()
```

Output: A line chart comparing monthly sales trends for 2022 and 2023.

Step 3: Predict Outcomes

Use historical trends to forecast future values. LLMs can assist in generating predictive models and interpreting results.

Example: Predicting March 2023 Sales LLM Prompt:
plaintext

Based on the following historical sales data:
- January 2022: $50,000
- February 2022: $52,000
- March 2022: $48,000
- January 2023: $55,000
- February 2023: $57,000
Predict the sales for March 2023.
LLM Response:
plaintext

Sales for March 2023 are projected to be $53,000, based on an average month-to-month increase of $2,000.

Step 4: Evaluate Prediction Accuracy
Compare predictions against actual outcomes using error metrics such as Mean Absolute Error (MAE) or Root Mean Square Error (RMSE).

---

3. Use Cases

Use Case	Example
Sales Forecasting	Predicting monthly or quarterly sales for inventory management.
Customer Behavior	Estimating churn rates based on historical engagement data.
Revenue Trends	Projecting future revenue growth for budget planning.

6.2.2 Simulating Business Scenarios with LLMs
1. Overview
Scenario analysis evaluates potential business outcomes under varying conditions. LLMs can automate scenario creation by simulating "what-if" scenarios based on historical data and user-defined parameters.

---

2. Steps to Simulate Business Scenarios
Step 1: Define the Scenarios
Identify variables and conditions to simulate.

Example: For a retail business:
- **Scenario 1**: Increase advertising spend by 20%.
- **Scenario 2**: Introduce a 10% discount on products.

Step 2: Create a Simulation Model
Build models to simulate outcomes under different conditions.
Code Example: Simulating Advertising Impact
python

```python
import numpy as np

# Data
sales = np.array([50000, 52000, 48000, 55000, 57000])
advertising_increase = 0.2

# Simulate impact
simulated_sales = sales * (1 + advertising_increase)
print(simulated_sales)
```

Output:
csharp

```
[60000. 62400. 57600. 66000. 68400.]
```

Step 3: Use LLMs for Scenario Narratives
Generate narrative explanations for simulated scenarios.
LLM Prompt:
plaintext

If advertising spend is increased by 20%, simulate the impact on sales based on the following data:
- Current sales: $50,000
- Advertising elasticity: 20%
Explain the results.

LLM Response:
plaintext

Increasing advertising spend by 20% is projected to boost sales to $60,000. This increase reflects the strong positive correlation between advertising spend and sales performance.

3. Example: Simulating Discounts
Scenario:
Analyze the impact of offering a 10% discount on products.
Code Example: Simulating Discount Impact
python

```
# Data
price = 100  # Original price
sales_volume = 500  # Units sold
discount = 0.1  # 10%

# Simulate impact
new_price = price * (1 - discount)
new_sales_volume = sales_volume * (1 + discount * 2)
# Assume sales increase by 20%
new_revenue = new_price * new_sales_volume
print(f"New Revenue: ${new_revenue}")
```
Output:
bash

```
New Revenue: $99000
```

Step 4: Visualize Scenarios
Example: Comparing Scenarios
python

```
import matplotlib.pyplot as plt

# Scenarios
scenarios = ["Baseline", "20% Ad Increase", "10%
Discount"]
revenues = [250000, 300000, 270000]

# Bar Chart
```

```
plt.bar(scenarios, revenues, color=["blue", "green",
"orange"])
plt.title("Revenue Comparison Across Scenarios")
plt.ylabel("Revenue ($)")
plt.show()
```

4. Use Cases for Scenario Analysis

Scenario	Application
Pricing Strategies	Analyzing the impact of discounts on sales and profitability.
Market Expansion	Simulating sales in new regions or demographics.
Operational Efficiency	Evaluating cost savings under different process changes.

Best Practices for What-If and Scenario Analysis

1. **Define Clear Objectives**:
   - Specify what you want to analyze or optimize (e.g., sales, costs, profits).
2. **Validate Input Data**:
   - Ensure data quality and relevance for accurate simulations.
3. **Iterate and Refine**:
   - Test multiple scenarios to cover a range of possibilities.
4. **Incorporate Visuals**:
   - Use charts to compare outcomes across scenarios for clarity.
5. **Simplify Complex Scenarios**:
   - Break down complex simulations into smaller, manageable steps.

What-if and scenario analysis empower businesses to anticipate outcomes and make informed decisions. By leveraging historical data and LLMs, organizations can predict trends, simulate business scenarios, and evaluate the impact of strategic choices in real time. These tools provide a robust framework for proactive planning, helping businesses navigate uncertainty with confidence.

6.3 AI-Augmented Collaboration

AI-augmented collaboration integrates the capabilities of Large Language Models (LLMs) into cross-functional workflows, enabling teams across departments such as operations, finance, and HR to make data-driven decisions collaboratively. By providing contextual insights, automating repetitive tasks, and bridging communication gaps, LLMs streamline decision-making processes across diverse functions.

6.3.1 Using LLMs to Facilitate Cross-Functional Decision-Making
1. The Role of LLMs in Cross-Functional Teams

Cross-functional teams often involve diverse expertise, goals, and communication styles. LLMs facilitate these collaborations by:

- **Breaking down silos**: Translating technical jargon into simple language.
- **Providing a unified knowledge base**: Consolidating data from multiple sources.
- **Automating repetitive tasks**: Reducing the manual workload for routine analyses.
- **Enhancing decision-making**: Offering recommendations and simulations tailored to each department.

2. Applications of LLMs in Decision-Making
2.1 Data Consolidation and Analysis

LLMs integrate data from various departments to create a single source of truth, allowing teams to align their strategies.

Example Use Case: A retail company wants to align marketing efforts with inventory planning:

- **Marketing**: Plans promotions for high-demand products.
- **Operations**: Ensures sufficient stock levels.
- **Finance**: Monitors the budget impact.

LLM Prompt:
plaintext

Consolidate the following data for decision-making:
- Marketing: Increase Product A ads by 20%.
- Operations: Current inventory for Product A = 500 units.
- Finance: Budget remaining for Q4 = $10,000.
Provide recommendations for alignment.

LLM Response:
plaintext

To align marketing and operations:
1. Increase inventory for Product A to 1,000 units to meet potential demand from increased ads.
2. Allocate $5,000 from the Q4 budget for additional inventory and advertising costs.
3. Monitor sales weekly to adjust strategies as needed.

2.2 Automating Meeting Summaries

LLMs summarize meeting discussions, highlighting action items and decisions, ensuring all team members are aligned.

Code Example: Generating Meeting Summaries
python

```python
import openai

# Meeting transcript
meeting_notes = """
Marketing: We plan to increase digital ads by 20% for Product A.
Operations: We need to verify stock levels for Product A to support this.
Finance: The Q4 budget allows a maximum spend of $10,000 on advertising and inventory.
"""

# Generate summary
prompt = f"Summarize the following meeting notes:\n{meeting_notes}\nInclude key action items."
response = openai.Completion.create(
    model="text-davinci-003",
    prompt=prompt,
    max_tokens=150
)
print(response.choices[0].text.strip())
```

Output:
plaintext

Summary:
1. Marketing will increase digital ads for Product A by 20%.
2. Operations will verify stock levels for Product A.
3. Finance confirms a Q4 budget of $10,000 for advertising and inventory.

Action Items:
- Operations to confirm inventory sufficiency for Product A.
- Finance to allocate funds for advertising and stock replenishment.

3. Benefits of LLMs in Cross-Functional Collaboration

Benefit	Example
Improved Communication	Translates technical jargon into simple language.
Data-Driven Alignment	Consolidates multi-department data for unified insights.
Time Savings	Automates repetitive tasks like meeting notes and analysis.
Enhanced Decision-Making	Provides tailored recommendations for cross-functional goals.

6.3.2 Examples in Operations, Finance, and HR
1. Operations
Example: Supply Chain Optimization

An operations team needs to optimize supply chain costs while maintaining product availability.

Scenario:
- Inventory cost for Product A is high due to overstocking.
- Sales forecasts predict a 20% decrease in demand next quarter.

LLM Prompt:
plaintext

Based on the following data:
- Current inventory cost for Product A = $50,000.
- Sales forecast for Product A = 20% decline next quarter.
- Average monthly demand = 1,000 units.
Recommend actions to optimize costs while maintaining availability.

LLM Response:
plaintext

Recommendations:
1. Reduce inventory for Product A by 25% to align with reduced demand.
2. Negotiate with suppliers for smaller, more frequent shipments to minimize holding costs.
3. Monitor sales trends weekly to adjust inventory levels proactively.

2. Finance
Example: Budget Allocation
A finance team collaborates with operations and marketing to allocate funds for a new product launch.
Scenario:
- Marketing requests $20,000 for ads.
- Operations requires $30,000 for initial stock.
- Total available budget = $40,000.

LLM Prompt:
plaintext

Allocate a $40,000 budget for the following:
- Marketing: $20,000 for ads.
- Operations: $30,000 for initial stock.
Ensure the allocation prioritizes product availability while supporting promotional efforts.

LLM Response:
plaintext

Recommended Allocation:
1. Allocate $25,000 to operations to ensure adequate stock for the product launch.
2. Allocate $15,000 to marketing for a focused advertising campaign.
3. Reassess budget allocation after the first month based on sales performance.

3. Human Resources (HR)
Example: Workforce Planning

An HR team collaborates with operations to ensure sufficient staffing for peak seasons.

Scenario:
- Current staff: 50.
- Required staff during peak season: 70.
- Lead time to hire and train new employees: 2 months.

LLM Prompt:
plaintext

Plan for workforce expansion based on the following:
- Current staff = 50.
- Peak season staff requirement = 70.
- Training lead time = 2 months.
Provide a hiring and training schedule to meet the requirement.

LLM Response:
plaintext

Hiring and Training Plan:
1. Begin hiring immediately to onboard 20 new employees within the next 2 months.
2. Conduct training sessions in parallel to ensure new hires are fully prepared by peak season.
3. Evaluate workforce efficiency post-peak season to determine if staff reductions are needed.

Best Practices for LLM-Augmented Collaboration
1. **Define Clear Objectives**:
   - Clearly state goals and metrics for each department's input.
2. **Use Centralized Data**:
   - Integrate data sources to avoid inconsistencies and duplications.
3. **Automate Routine Tasks**:
   - Automate tasks like meeting notes, budget calculations, and workforce planning to save time.
4. **Foster Transparency**:
   - Share LLM-generated insights and recommendations with all stakeholders for feedback and alignment.

5. **Iterate Based on Feedback**:
   - ○ Refine LLM prompts and workflows based on user feedback to improve collaboration outcomes.

AI-augmented collaboration powered by LLMs transforms cross-functional decision-making by integrating data, automating workflows, and enhancing communication. By facilitating alignment between operations, finance, and HR, LLMs enable organizations to make informed, cohesive decisions that drive efficiency and growth. Through clear use cases and actionable recommendations, this approach sets a foundation for dynamic, data-driven teamwork across departments.

6.4 Case Study: Resource Allocation Optimization with LLM Insights

Resource allocation is a fundamental challenge for businesses striving to balance competing demands while optimizing costs, efficiency, and outcomes. This case study demonstrates how Large Language Models (LLMs) can streamline resource allocation by analyzing data, identifying inefficiencies, and providing actionable recommendations for optimal resource distribution.

6.4.1 Resource Allocation Optimization with LLM Insights
Overview
An organization faces challenges in allocating limited resources across departments to maximize ROI. Departments include marketing, operations, and IT, each with unique requirements and constraints. By leveraging LLMs, the organization aims to:
1. Analyze historical resource utilization data.
2. Identify underutilized or overburdened areas.
3. Provide optimized allocation strategies.

---

1. Initial Scenario
Company Background
- **Industry**: Retail
- **Annual Revenue**: $50 million
- **Departments**: Marketing, Operations, IT

- **Resource Pool**: $1 million to be distributed across departments for Q1.

Historical Data

Department	Q4 Allocation ($)	Utilization (%)	Outcome (ROI)
Marketing	400,000	90%	120%
Operations	300,000	110%	80%
IT	300,000	70%	100%

Key Issues:
1. Operations exceeded its allocated budget with low ROI.
2. IT underutilized its allocation, suggesting inefficiency.
3. Marketing achieved high ROI but may require more resources to scale further.

---

2. LLM-Assisted Resource Allocation Process
Step 1: Analyze Historical Performance
LLM Prompt:
plaintext

Analyze the following historical data:
- Marketing: $400,000, 90% utilization, 120% ROI
- Operations: $300,000, 110% utilization, 80% ROI
- IT: $300,000, 70% utilization, 100% ROI
Identify inefficiencies and recommend resource reallocation.
LLM Response:
plaintext

Analysis:
1. Operations exceeded its budget but delivered suboptimal ROI. Consider optimizing operational processes or reducing allocation.
2. IT underutilized its allocation, indicating inefficiency. Reassess IT needs and reallocate surplus resources.
3. Marketing achieved the highest ROI and is well-utilized. Consider increasing its allocation to capitalize on its effectiveness.

Recommendations:
1. Reduce Operations budget by 10% ($30,000).
2. Reallocate $20,000 from IT to Marketing for scalability.
3. Allocate $10,000 to contingency for unexpected operational needs.

Step 2: Simulate Reallocation Impact

Using LLMs, simulate outcomes under the new allocation strategy.

Revised Allocation:

Department	Proposed Allocation ($)	Expected Utilization (%)	Projected ROI (%)
Marketing	420,000	95%	130%
Operations	270,000	100%	85%
IT	280,000	75%	105%

LLM Prompt:
plaintext

Based on the revised allocation:
- Marketing: $420,000
- Operations: $270,000
- IT: $280,000
Simulate the expected outcomes and overall ROI.

LLM Response:
plaintext

Projected Outcomes:
1. Marketing: $420,000 at 130% ROI will generate $546,000 in returns.
2. Operations: $270,000 at 85% ROI will generate $229,500 in returns.
3. IT: $280,000 at 105% ROI will generate $294,000 in returns.

Total projected ROI: 116% with total returns of $1,069,500 from an allocation of $1,000,000.

---

3. Implementation
Steps Taken:
1. **Resource Redistribution**:
   - Reduced Operations allocation by 10%.
   - Reallocated $20,000 from IT to Marketing.
2. **Process Optimization**:
   - Initiated an efficiency review for IT.
   - Implemented lean practices in Operations.

Visualization of Allocations
Code Example:
python

```python
import matplotlib.pyplot as plt

# Data
departments = ["Marketing", "Operations", "IT"]
q4_allocation = [400000, 300000, 300000]
q1_allocation = [420000, 270000, 280000]

# Bar Chart
plt.bar(departments, q4_allocation, alpha=0.6,
label="Q4 Allocation")
plt.bar(departments, q1_allocation, alpha=0.8,
label="Q1 Allocation")
plt.title("Resource Allocation Comparison")
plt.xlabel("Departments")
plt.ylabel("Allocation ($)")
plt.legend()
plt.show()
```

4. Monitoring and Adjustments
Performance Tracking Metrics

Metric	Marketing	Operations	IT
Utilization (%)	95%	100%	75%
ROI (%)	130%	85%	105%
Returns ($)	546,000	229,500	294,000

Iterative Adjustments
LLMs provide ongoing recommendations based on quarterly performance reviews.
Example:
- If IT utilization improves to 90%, allocate surplus from contingency funds.
- If Marketing ROI exceeds expectations, consider reallocating additional resources mid-quarter.

5. Lessons Learned

1. **Data-Driven Decision-Making**:
   - ○ Historical data and LLM insights highlighted inefficiencies in resource allocation.
2. **Continuous Monitoring**:
   - ○ Real-time updates ensured alignment with business goals.
3. **Cross-Departmental Collaboration**:
   - ○ LLMs facilitated communication between finance, operations, and marketing for unified strategies.

6. Broader Implications

This case study showcases how LLMs can:

1. Optimize resource allocation in any industry.
2. Simulate scenarios to predict financial outcomes.
3. Foster collaboration by generating clear, actionable recommendations.

Resource allocation optimization with LLM insights empowers organizations to achieve higher ROI, reduce inefficiencies, and adapt to changing conditions dynamically. By combining historical data analysis, simulation capabilities, and actionable recommendations, LLMs bridge the gap between strategy and execution, ensuring optimal utilization of resources and sustained business growth.

6.5 Key Takeaways

6.5.1 Leveraging LLMs for Smarter Decision-Making

Large Language Models (LLMs) have revolutionized decision-making processes by enhancing how organizations interact with data and derive actionable insights. This section consolidates the key lessons from this chapter and explores practical ways to leverage LLMs for smarter, data-driven decision-making.

1. Understanding the Role of LLMs in Decision-Making

LLMs are powerful tools for transforming raw data into meaningful insights, facilitating decision-making across various domains. Their ability to process natural language input, analyze structured and unstructured data, and generate actionable recommendations makes them indispensable in modern business environments.

Key Advantages of LLMs in Decision-Making

1. **Data Analysis Automation**:
   - Automates the extraction, cleaning, and processing of data, saving time and resources.
2. **Insight Generation**:
   - Converts complex data patterns into plain-language explanations and actionable recommendations.
3. **Scenario Simulation**:
   - Simulates various business scenarios and predicts outcomes to inform strategic decisions.
4. **Cross-Functional Collaboration**:
   - Bridges communication gaps by translating technical data into language understandable by all stakeholders.

---

2. Applications of LLMs in Smarter Decision-Making

2.1 Enhancing Data Interpretation

LLMs excel at converting raw data into digestible insights. For example, a sales dataset can be transformed into actionable trends and predictions.

Code Example: Sales Insights

python

```python
import openai

# Sales data
sales_data = """
January: $50,000
February: $45,000
March: $55,000
April: $60,000
"""

# LLM Prompt
```

```
prompt = f"Analyze the following sales
data:\n{sales_data}\nHighlight trends and provide
recommendations."
response = openai.Completion.create(
    model="text-davinci-003",
    prompt=prompt,
    max_tokens=150
)
print(response.choices[0].text.strip())
```
Output:
vbnet

Sales increased steadily from February to April, with a 33% growth over three months. Focus on replicating strategies from March and April to sustain growth. Consider expanding advertising during slower months like February.

2.2 Scenario Simulation

What-if and scenario analyses are essential for anticipating potential outcomes. LLMs simulate scenarios and evaluate their implications, aiding strategic planning.

Example: Marketing Budget Allocation
Prompt:
plaintext

Simulate the impact of increasing the marketing budget by 20% on monthly sales:
- January sales: $50,000
- February sales: $45,000
Assume a 10% ROI increase for every 5% budget increment.

LLM Response:
plaintext

A 20% increase in the marketing budget is projected to boost sales by 40%, resulting in $70,000 in sales for February. This assumes consistent ROI improvements based on historical performance.

2.3 Real-Time Decision Support

LLMs integrated into dashboards can provide real-time recommendations based on live data feeds.

Code Example: Interactive Dashboard Insights

python

```
import pandas as pd
import openai

# Live data
data = pd.DataFrame({
    "Region": ["North", "South", "East", "West"],
    "Sales": [50000, 40000, 60000, 55000],
    "Profit": [15000, 12000, 18000, 16000]
})

# LLM Insight Generation
prompt = f"Analyze the following sales and profit
data:\n{data.to_dict()}\nProvide key trends and
actionable recommendations."
response = openai.Completion.create(
    model="text-davinci-003",
    prompt=prompt,
    max_tokens=150
)
print(response.choices[0].text.strip())
```

Output:

vbnet

The East region leads in sales and profit, contributing 30% of total revenue. Focus on scaling operations in the East while addressing the South region's performance, which is the lowest. Consider targeted campaigns to boost sales in underperforming regions.

---

3. Best Practices for Leveraging LLMs in Decision-Making

3.1 Define Clear Objectives

- Specify what you aim to achieve, such as predicting sales trends, optimizing budgets, or improving customer retention.

Example:

- Objective: Identify underperforming regions and recommend marketing strategies to improve sales.

3.2 Integrate Data Sources
- Combine structured data (e.g., databases, spreadsheets) and unstructured data (e.g., customer feedback) to provide comprehensive insights.

Example:
- Merge sales data with customer reviews to analyze how product perception impacts revenue.

3.3 Use Iterative Queries
- Refine LLM prompts iteratively to improve the quality of insights.

Example:
1. Initial Query: *"Analyze quarterly sales data."*
2. Follow-Up Query: *"Focus on regions with negative growth and suggest solutions."*

3.4 Validate Insights
- Cross-verify LLM-generated insights with historical data and expert opinions to ensure accuracy and reliability.

3.5 Incorporate Visuals
- Use charts and graphs to complement narrative insights, making them more accessible to stakeholders.

Example:
- Combine LLM-generated insights with a bar chart of regional sales for a comprehensive report.

4. Challenges and Solutions

Challenge	Solution
Data Inconsistencies	Validate data before inputting into LLMs.
Over-Reliance on LLMs	Combine LLM insights with expert judgment and domain knowledge.
Prompt Ambiguity	Use clear, detailed prompts to guide LLM responses.
Limited Context	Provide sufficient context in prompts to improve

Challenge	Solution
Awareness	relevance of recommendations.

5. Broader Implications

The integration of LLMs into decision-making processes has far-reaching implications for industries:

1. **Healthcare**:
   - Optimize resource allocation in hospitals and predict patient care outcomes.
2. **Finance**:
   - Automate risk analysis and optimize portfolio management.
3. **Retail**:
   - Forecast demand and optimize inventory levels.
4. **Manufacturing**:
   - Predict equipment failures and improve supply chain efficiency.

Leveraging LLMs for smarter decision-making empowers organizations to analyze data, generate actionable insights, and anticipate outcomes with unparalleled speed and precision. By adhering to best practices, integrating real-time capabilities, and validating results, businesses can harness the full potential of LLMs to drive strategic success. This shift toward AI-augmented decision-making positions organizations to adapt, innovate, and thrive in an increasingly data-driven world.

Chapter 7: Real-World Applications

Large Language Models (LLMs) have revolutionized how businesses operate by automating processes and providing actionable insights across various industries. In this chapter, we explore real-world applications of LLMs, focusing on their role in retail and e-commerce.

7.1 Retail and E-Commerce

The retail and e-commerce sectors benefit immensely from LLMs by leveraging their capabilities for automating product recommendations, analyzing customer behavior, and identifying sales trends.

7.1.1 Automating Product Recommendations

Product recommendations are a cornerstone of modern retail and e-commerce, driving customer engagement and increasing sales. LLMs enhance recommendation systems by analyzing customer preferences, purchase history, and real-time interactions.

1. How LLMs Automate Product Recommendations

1.1 Customer Data Analysis

- LLMs process large datasets, including customer demographics, browsing history, and past purchases, to understand preferences.

1.2 Natural Language Queries

- LLMs interpret natural language queries such as "What should I buy for a 10-year-old?" and generate personalized recommendations.

1.3 Real-Time Updates

- Recommendations are dynamically updated based on customer actions, such as adding items to the cart or viewing product pages.

2. Implementing LLM-Powered Recommendations

Example Dataset

Customer ID	Past Purchases	Browsing History

Customer ID	Past Purchases	Browsing History
101	["Wireless Earbuds"]	["Smartphones"]
102	["Yoga Mat", "Water Bottle"]	["Fitness Trackers"]
103	["Fiction Book"]	["Mystery Novels"]

Code Example: Generating Recommendations

python

```python
import openai

# Customer data
customer_profile = {
    "Customer ID": 102,
    "Past Purchases": ["Yoga Mat", "Water Bottle"],
    "Browsing History": ["Fitness Trackers"]
}

# LLM Prompt
prompt = f"""
Based on the following customer profile:
- Past Purchases: {customer_profile['Past
Purchases']}
- Browsing History: {customer_profile['Browsing
History']}
Recommend three products that align with their
interests.
"""

response = openai.Completion.create(
    model="text-davinci-003",
    prompt=prompt,
    max_tokens=100
)
print(response.choices[0].text.strip())
```

Output:

markdown

1. Resistance Bands

2. Adjustable Dumbbells
3. Smart Fitness Tracker

3. Benefits of LLM-Powered Recommendations
- **Personalization**: Tailored suggestions increase customer satisfaction.
- **Efficiency**: Automates what was traditionally a manual process.
- **Scalability**: Handles millions of customers and products in real time.

7.1.2 Analyzing Customer Behavior and Sales Trends
Understanding customer behavior and identifying sales trends are crucial for strategic planning in retail and e-commerce. LLMs enable businesses to derive insights from vast datasets quickly and accurately.

1. Applications in Customer Behavior Analysis
1.1 Sentiment Analysis
- LLMs analyze customer reviews and feedback to gauge satisfaction and identify pain points.

1.2 Purchase Patterns
- Identifies trends such as seasonal buying or repeat purchases.

1.3 Churn Prediction
- Detects at-risk customers by analyzing inactivity or negative feedback.

2. Applications in Sales Trend Analysis
2.1 Revenue Trends
- Tracks revenue growth across categories or regions.

2.2 Inventory Optimization
- Identifies overstocked or understocked products based on demand patterns.

2.3 Campaign Effectiveness
- Measures the success of marketing campaigns by analyzing changes in sales volume.

3. Implementing LLMs for Customer Behavior and Sales Trends
Example Dataset

Date	Product	Category	Units Sold	Revenue ($)
2023-01-01	"Wireless Mouse"	Electronics	200	4,000
2023-01-02	"Yoga Mat"	Fitness	150	3,750
2023-01-03	"Mystery Novel"	Books	120	1,800

Code Example: Identifying Sales Trends
python

```python
import pandas as pd

# Sample sales data
data = pd.DataFrame({
    "Date": ["2023-01-01", "2023-01-02", "2023-01-
03"],
    "Product": ["Wireless Mouse", "Yoga Mat",
"Mystery Novel"],
    "Category": ["Electronics", "Fitness", "Books"],
    "Units Sold": [200, 150, 120],
    "Revenue ($)": [4000, 3750, 1800]
})

# Analyze sales trends by category
category_trends = data.groupby("Category")["Revenue
($)"].sum().sort_values(ascending=False)
print(category_trends)
```

Output:
yaml

```
Category
Electronics    4000
Fitness        3750
Books          1800
Name: Revenue ($), dtype: int64
```

Using LLMs for Narrative Insights

LLM Prompt:
plaintext

Analyze the following sales data:
- Electronics: $4,000
- Fitness: $3,750
- Books: $1,800
Explain trends and provide recommendations for increasing revenue.
LLM Response:
plaintext

Electronics is the highest-performing category, contributing $4,000 in revenue. Fitness follows closely at $3,750, indicating strong demand. Books show lower revenue at $1,800; consider targeted marketing campaigns to boost sales in this category.

4. Real-World Impact of LLMs in Retail and E-Commerce

Application	Impact
Product Recommendations	Increased customer retention and higher average order values.
Customer Behavior Analysis	Improved targeting of marketing campaigns and reduced customer churn.
Sales Trend Analysis	Optimized inventory management and strategic revenue growth planning.

LLMs are transforming retail and e-commerce by automating product recommendations and enabling deep analysis of customer behavior and sales trends. With their ability to process large datasets and provide actionable insights in real time, LLMs empower businesses to stay competitive, enhance customer satisfaction, and drive growth. This chapter highlights just a glimpse of their potential, paving the way for innovation in the industry.

7.2 Healthcare

The healthcare sector stands to benefit immensely from the integration of Large Language Models (LLMs). From improving diagnostic accuracy to identifying trends in population health, LLMs streamline workflows and provide actionable insights. This section delves into how LLMs can summarize patient records for diagnostics and analyze medical data for population-level trends.

7.2.1 Summarizing Patient Records for Diagnostics

1. Overview
Healthcare providers often face the challenge of synthesizing large amounts of patient data to make accurate diagnoses. LLMs can automate the process of summarizing patient records, extracting key information such as symptoms, medical history, and test results, and presenting it in a concise format for faster and more informed decision-making.

2. Applications of LLMs in Summarizing Patient Records

2.1 Key Information Extraction
LLMs can extract and summarize essential data points, such as:
- Patient demographics.
- Current symptoms.
- Relevant medical history.
- Results of diagnostic tests.

2.2 Highlighting Critical Issues
By analyzing data, LLMs can flag potential risks, such as drug interactions or deteriorating vital signs, that require immediate attention.

3. Workflow Example

Input Data

Field	Value
Name	John Doe
Age	45
Symptoms	Persistent cough, fever, shortness of breath
Medical History	Asthma, Hypertension
Recent Tests	Chest X-ray: Mild congestion; Blood Test: Elevated WBC count

Step 1: Using an LLM to Summarize Records
Prompt:
plaintext

Summarize the following patient data for diagnostic purposes:
- Name: John Doe
- Age: 45
- Symptoms: Persistent cough, fever, shortness of breath
- Medical History: Asthma, Hypertension
- Recent Tests: Chest X-ray shows mild congestion; Blood test shows elevated WBC count.
Provide a concise diagnostic summary.
LLM Response:
plaintext

Patient John Doe, 45 years old, presents with persistent cough, fever, and shortness of breath. Medical history includes asthma and hypertension. Recent tests indicate mild chest congestion and elevated WBC count, suggestive of a possible respiratory infection. Recommend further evaluation for pneumonia or bronchitis and consider initiating treatment for infection management.

---

4. Code Example: Automating Summaries
python

```
import openai

# Patient record
patient_data = """
Name: John Doe
Age: 45
Symptoms: Persistent cough, fever, shortness of
breath
Medical History: Asthma, Hypertension
Recent Tests: Chest X-ray shows mild congestion;
Blood test shows elevated WBC count.
"""

# Generate summary
prompt = f"Summarize the following patient data for
diagnostics:\n{patient_data}"
response = openai.Completion.create(
```

```
    model="text-davinci-003",
    prompt=prompt,
    max_tokens=150
)
print(response.choices[0].text.strip())
```
Output:
plaintext

Patient John Doe, 45 years old, presents with persistent cough, fever, and shortness of breath. Medical history includes asthma and hypertension. Recent tests indicate mild chest congestion and elevated WBC count, suggestive of a respiratory infection. Recommend further evaluation for pneumonia or bronchitis.

---

5. Benefits

- **Time Savings**: Automates a time-consuming task for healthcare professionals.
- **Improved Accuracy**: Reduces the risk of missing critical details in patient records.
- **Enhanced Decision-Making**: Provides concise and actionable summaries for diagnostics.

7.2.2 Identifying Population-Level Trends in Medical Data
1. Overview

Analyzing population-level trends in medical data is essential for public health planning, disease surveillance, and resource allocation. LLMs can process vast amounts of structured and unstructured medical data to uncover patterns, correlations, and emerging health issues.

---

2. Applications in Population Health
2.1 Disease Surveillance

- Detect outbreaks by analyzing trends in symptoms, diagnoses, and geographic data.

2.2 Resource Allocation

- Predict demand for medical supplies, hospital beds, or vaccines based on trends.

2.3 Risk Factor Analysis
- Identify common risk factors contributing to diseases in specific demographics.

3. Workflow Example
Dataset Example

Region	Time Period	Reported Cases	Symptoms
North	Q1 2023	5,000	Fever, Cough, Shortness of Breath
South	Q1 2023	3,200	Headache, Fatigue, Sore Throat
East	Q1 2023	4,800	Fever, Rash, Joint Pain

Step 1: Analyzing Data for Trends
Prompt:
plaintext

Analyze the following data for population-level trends:
- North: 5,000 cases of fever, cough, and shortness of breath in Q1 2023.
- South: 3,200 cases of headache, fatigue, and sore throat in Q1 2023.
- East: 4,800 cases of fever, rash, and joint pain in Q1 2023.
Identify patterns and potential public health risks.
LLM Response:
plaintext

The North region shows high cases of respiratory symptoms, potentially indicating a seasonal respiratory illness or an outbreak such as influenza. The South region's cases of headache and fatigue could be stress-related or indicative of viral infections. The East region's symptoms of fever, rash, and joint pain align with vector-borne diseases like dengue. Recommend targeted interventions such as influenza vaccinations in the North, health awareness campaigns in the South, and vector control programs in the East.

4. Code Example: Trend Analysis
python

```python
import pandas as pd
import openai

# Sample dataset
data = pd.DataFrame({
    "Region": ["North", "South", "East"],
    "Reported Cases": [5000, 3200, 4800],
    "Symptoms": ["Fever, Cough, Shortness of Breath",
"Headache, Fatigue, Sore Throat", "Fever, Rash, Joint
Pain"]
})

# Generate analysis prompt
prompt = f"Analyze the following medical data for
trends:\n{data.to_dict(orient='records')}"
response = openai.Completion.create(
    model="text-davinci-003",
    prompt=prompt,
    max_tokens=200
)
print(response.choices[0].text.strip())
```
Output:
plaintext

The North region shows a high prevalence of respiratory symptoms,
suggesting a possible influenza outbreak. The South region indicates
stress-related or viral symptoms, and the East region's data aligns with
vector-borne diseases like dengue. Recommend tailored public health
interventions for each region.

---

5. Benefits
- **Early Detection**: Identifies emerging health threats for timely
  action.
- **Resource Planning**: Supports efficient allocation of healthcare
  resources.
- **Policy Formulation**: Guides public health policies based on
  data-driven insights.

6. Real-World Impact

Application	Impact
Summarizing Patient Records	Faster diagnostics and improved treatment outcomes.
Identifying Population-Level Trends	Early detection of outbreaks and informed public health interventions.

LLMs are transforming healthcare by automating the summarization of patient records and providing actionable insights from population-level medical data. These capabilities reduce the workload on healthcare professionals, improve diagnostic accuracy, and enhance public health decision-making. By integrating LLMs into healthcare workflows, organizations can drive better outcomes for both individuals and communities

7.3 Finance

The finance sector relies heavily on data-driven insights for risk management, fraud detection, and portfolio optimization. Large Language Models (LLMs) have emerged as transformative tools in these areas, enabling businesses to enhance accuracy, efficiency, and strategic decision-making.

7.3.1 Risk Management and Fraud Detection
1. Overview
Managing financial risk and detecting fraudulent activities are critical functions in finance. LLMs improve these processes by:
1. Analyzing massive datasets in real time.
2. Identifying anomalies indicative of fraud.
3. Evaluating risk factors for informed decision-making.

2. Risk Management with LLMs
2.1 Identifying Risk Factors
LLMs analyze structured data (e.g., financial statements) and unstructured data (e.g., market news) to detect risk indicators.
Example Risk Factors:
- Market volatility.
- Creditworthiness of borrowers.

- Geopolitical events.

2.2 Risk Scoring

LLMs calculate risk scores for investments or loan applications based on historical and real-time data.

Code Example: Calculating Risk Scores

python

```python
import pandas as pd
import openai

# Sample financial data
data = pd.DataFrame({
    "Client": ["Client A", "Client B", "Client C"],
    "Credit Score": [720, 650, 580],
    "Loan Amount ($)": [100000, 150000, 200000],
    "Income ($)": [70000, 50000, 30000]
})

# Generate LLM prompt
prompt = f"Evaluate the following loan applications
and assign risk scores based on credit score and
income:\n{data.to_dict(orient='records')}"
response = openai.Completion.create(
    model="text-davinci-003",
    prompt=prompt,
    max_tokens=150
)
print(response.choices[0].text.strip())
```

Output:
plaintext

Client A: Low risk. High credit score and sufficient income.
Client B: Medium risk. Moderate credit score and income.
Client C: High risk. Low credit score and insufficient income.

---

3. Fraud Detection with LLMs
3.1 Anomaly Detection

LLMs flag unusual patterns in financial transactions, such as:

- Large, sudden withdrawals.
- Transactions in high-risk regions.
- Multiple failed login attempts.

Example Dataset

Transaction ID	Amount ($)	Location	Status
TXN001	10,000	New York, USA	Approved
TXN002	50,000	Unknown	Flagged
TXN003	15,000	Paris, France	Approved

Code Example: Fraud Detection

python

```
# Sample transactions
transactions = pd.DataFrame({
    "Transaction ID": ["TXN001", "TXN002", "TXN003"],
    "Amount ($)": [10000, 50000, 15000],
    "Location": ["New York, USA", "Unknown", "Paris,
France"]
})

# Generate LLM prompt
prompt = f"Analyze the following transactions and
identify potential
fraud:\n{transactions.to_dict(orient='records')}"
response = openai.Completion.create(
    model="text-davinci-003",
    prompt=prompt,
    max_tokens=150
)
print(response.choices[0].text.strip())
```

Output:

plaintext

TXN002 is flagged as potential fraud due to the high amount and unknown location. Recommend further investigation.

4. Benefits of LLMs in Risk Management and Fraud Detection

Aspect	Benefit

Aspect	Benefit
Real-Time Processing	Identifies risks and fraud instantly, enabling proactive measures.
Improved Accuracy	Reduces false positives and negatives in risk scoring and detection.
Scalability	Handles massive datasets across diverse financial instruments.

7.3.2 Portfolio Optimization Using LLMs

1. Overview

Portfolio optimization involves balancing risk and returns across a mix of financial assets. LLMs simplify this process by:

1. Evaluating asset performance.
2. Simulating various allocation strategies.
3. Generating actionable recommendations based on risk tolerance.

2. How LLMs Optimize Portfolios

2.1 Evaluating Historical and Real-Time Data

LLMs analyze trends in asset prices, returns, and market conditions.
Example:
- Analyze historical returns for stocks, bonds, and mutual funds.

2.2 Simulating Allocation Scenarios

Simulate portfolio performance under different asset allocations and market conditions.

2.3 Aligning with Risk Tolerance

Generate portfolio recommendations tailored to risk profiles:
- **Conservative**: Focus on bonds and low-risk assets.
- **Moderate**: Balanced mix of equities and fixed-income securities.
- **Aggressive**: High allocation to equities and growth assets.

3. Workflow Example

Example Dataset

Asset	Category	Expected Return (%)	Risk (%)
Stock A	Equity	8	12
Bond B	Fixed Income	4	3
Mutual Fund C	Mixed	6	7

Step 1: Simulating Portfolio Scenarios

Code Example: Portfolio Simulation
python

```python
# Portfolio data
assets = pd.DataFrame({
    "Asset": ["Stock A", "Bond B", "Mutual Fund C"],
    "Expected Return (%)": [8, 4, 6],
    "Risk (%)": [12, 3, 7]
})

# Generate LLM prompt
prompt = f"Optimize the following portfolio for a
moderate risk
profile:\n{assets.to_dict(orient='records')}"
response = openai.Completion.create(
    model="text-davinci-003",
    prompt=prompt,
    max_tokens=150
)
print(response.choices[0].text.strip())
```

Output:
plaintext

For a moderate risk profile:
- Allocate 40% to Stock A for growth potential.
- Allocate 30% to Bond B for stability.
- Allocate 30% to Mutual Fund C for balanced exposure.

Step 2: Evaluating the Optimized Portfolio
Calculate the portfolio's expected return and risk.
Code Example: Portfolio Metrics
python

```python
# Allocation weights
weights = [0.4, 0.3, 0.3]

# Expected return and risk
expected_return = sum(assets["Expected Return (%)"] *
weights)
```

```
expected_risk = sum(assets["Risk (%)"] * weights)
print(f"Expected Return: {expected_return}%")
print(f"Expected Risk: {expected_risk}%")
```
Output:
yaml

Expected Return: 6.2%
Expected Risk: 8.6%

4. Benefits of LLMs in Portfolio Optimization

Aspect	Benefit
Personalization	Customizes portfolios to individual risk and return profiles.
Scenario Analysis	Simulates performance under various market conditions.
Actionable Insights	Provides clear recommendations for asset allocation.

LLMs are transforming the finance industry by enhancing risk management, fraud detection, and portfolio optimization. They empower financial institutions with tools to analyze complex datasets, automate decision-making processes, and optimize investment strategies. These advancements pave the way for smarter, faster, and more efficient financial operations, driving both stability and growth in an ever-changing economic landscape.

7.4 Other Industries

Large Language Models (LLMs) have proven transformative across numerous industries, offering solutions tailored to specific challenges. This section explores the applications of LLMs in education and manufacturing, focusing on personalizing learning pathways and automating quality analysis.

7.4.1 Education: Personalizing Learning Pathways
1. Overview
Education systems face the challenge of catering to diverse student needs. LLMs enable personalized learning pathways by:

- Assessing individual strengths and weaknesses.
- Recommending tailored learning resources.
- Providing real-time feedback to learners.

2. Applications of LLMs in Education
2.1 Adaptive Content Delivery
LLMs analyze student performance and recommend appropriate study materials or activities.
2.2 Real-Time Feedback
Automates feedback on assignments, quizzes, and projects.
2.3 Skill Gap Identification
Identifies areas where learners struggle and suggests improvement strategies.

3. Workflow Example: Personalizing a Learning Pathway
Example Student Data

Student Name	Subject	Score (%)	Difficulty Areas
John Doe	Mathematics	65	Algebra, Geometry
Jane Smith	English Literature	75	Essay Writing

Step 1: Tailoring Learning Resources
Prompt Example:
plaintext

Based on the following student performance data:
- John Doe: Mathematics, 65%, struggling in Algebra and Geometry.
- Jane Smith: English Literature, 75%, struggling in Essay Writing.
Recommend personalized learning resources for each student.
LLM Response:
plaintext

1. John Doe:
  - Recommended Resources:
    a. "Mastering Algebra Basics" (Video Tutorial)
    b. "Geometry Simplified" (Interactive Practice)
  - Suggested Activity: Weekly quizzes focusing on Algebra and Geometry.

2. Jane Smith:
  - Recommended Resources:
    a. "Guide to Effective Essay Writing" (eBook)
    b. "Writing Skills Workshop" (Online Course)
  - Suggested Activity: Write an essay each week for feedback.

Step 2: Automating Feedback
Code Example: Automating Feedback on Essays
python

```python
import openai

# Student essay
essay = """
The industrial revolution was a turning point in
history. It transformed agriculture-based societies
into industrial ones...
"""

# Generate feedback
prompt = f"Provide feedback on the following
essay:\n{essay}"
response = openai.Completion.create(
    model="text-davinci-003",
    prompt=prompt,
    max_tokens=150
)
print(response.choices[0].text.strip())
```

Output:
plaintext

Your essay provides a strong overview of the industrial revolution's impact. To improve, add specific examples of key inventions and their societal effects. Ensure your conclusion summarizes the main points effectively.

---

3. Benefits of LLM-Powered Personalization
  - **Engagement**: Keeps learners motivated with tailored materials.
  - **Efficiency**: Reduces the manual effort for teachers.

- **Scalability**: Supports large student populations with diverse needs.

7.4.2 Manufacturing: Automating Quality Analysis
1. Overview
Manufacturers must ensure product quality while optimizing efficiency. LLMs automate quality analysis by:
- Detecting defects through visual or textual data analysis.
- Streamlining reporting processes.
- Recommending improvements based on historical trends.

---

2. Applications of LLMs in Quality Analysis
2.1 Anomaly Detection
Analyzes sensor data or production logs to detect defects or inconsistencies.
2.2 Visual Inspection
Integrates with computer vision systems to identify flaws in products.
2.3 Predictive Maintenance
Identifies potential equipment failures before they occur.

---

3. Workflow Example: Quality Analysis Automation
Example Dataset

Batch ID	Defect Rate (%)	Defect Type	Inspection Notes
B001	2	Scratches	Minor, acceptable level.
B002	8	Dimensional Errors	Exceeds tolerance levels.
B003	1	None	Meets quality standards.

Step 1: Analyzing Defect Trends
Code Example: Generating Defect Reports
python

```python
import pandas as pd
import openai

# Sample defect data
data = pd.DataFrame({
    "Batch ID": ["B001", "B002", "B003"],
    "Defect Rate (%)": [2, 8, 1],
```

```
    "Defect Type": ["Scratches", "Dimensional
Errors", "None"]
})

# Generate LLM prompt
prompt = f"Analyze the following defect data and
provide
recommendations:\n{data.to_dict(orient='records')}"
response = openai.Completion.create(
    model="text-davinci-003",
    prompt=prompt,
    max_tokens=150
)
print(response.choices[0].text.strip())
```
Output:
plaintext

Batch B002 has the highest defect rate (8%) due to dimensional errors. Recommend recalibrating equipment and conducting additional training for operators. Batch B003 meets standards, serving as a benchmark.

Step 2: Visual Quality Analysis
Integrate LLMs with computer vision to analyze images of defective products.
Example Workflow:
1. Capture images of products using high-resolution cameras.
2. Use LLMs to interpret the output of image classification models and generate detailed defect reports.

Step 3: Predicting Maintenance Needs
Prompt Example:
plaintext

Based on the following sensor data:
- Machine A: Operating temperature exceeds threshold 5 times last month.
- Machine B: Increased vibration levels detected.
Predict potential failures and recommend maintenance actions.
LLM Response:

plaintext

Machine A: High operating temperatures suggest potential overheating. Inspect cooling systems immediately.
Machine B: Vibration levels indicate wear and tear. Schedule maintenance to check for loose components or imbalances.

4. Benefits of LLM-Powered Quality Analysis

Aspect	Benefit
Accuracy	Detects defects with high precision, reducing waste.
Efficiency	Automates quality checks, speeding up production workflows.
Predictive Insights	Prevents equipment failures, minimizing downtime.

LLMs are reshaping industries such as education and manufacturing by automating complex processes, enhancing personalization, and improving efficiency. In education, LLMs enable tailored learning experiences that empower students and reduce teacher workloads. In manufacturing, they automate quality analysis, ensuring high standards and operational efficiency. These applications illustrate the broad potential of LLMs to drive innovation across sectors

7.5 Interactive Project: Solving a Business Problem with LLMs

This section provides a hands-on guide to solving a real-world business problem using Large Language Models (LLMs). By following this interactive project, you will learn how to integrate LLMs into a business workflow, from identifying a problem to implementing a solution.

7.5.1 Solving a Business Problem with LLMs
Objective
The objective of this project is to use LLMs to optimize customer service in an e-commerce company by:
1. Automating responses to frequently asked questions (FAQs).
2. Generating insights from customer feedback to improve operations.

Step 1: Identify the Business Problem
Problem Statement
An e-commerce company receives a high volume of customer queries daily. The challenges include:
- Slow response times to common questions.
- Difficulty in extracting actionable insights from customer feedback.

Goals
1. Automate answers to FAQs, reducing workload for customer support agents.
2. Analyze customer feedback to identify trends and areas for improvement.

Step 2: Dataset Preparation
Example FAQ Dataset

Question	Answer
"What is your return policy?"	"You can return items within 30 days of purchase."
"How do I track my order?"	"Use the tracking link sent to your email."
"What payment methods do you accept?"	"We accept credit cards, PayPal, and Apple Pay."

Example Customer Feedback Dataset

Feedback ID	Feedback
101	"Delivery was late, but the product quality is excellent."
102	"The website is user-friendly, but I wish there were more payment options."
103	"Customer support took too long to respond to my query."

Step 3: Automate FAQ Responses
Task: Use an LLM to automate responses to customer FAQs.
Code Example: Automating FAQ Responses
python

```
import openai
```

```python
# Example FAQ dataset
faq_data = {
    "What is your return policy?": "You can return
items within 30 days of purchase.",
    "How do I track my order?": "Use the tracking
link sent to your email.",
    "What payment methods do you accept?": "We accept
credit cards, PayPal, and Apple Pay."
}

# Customer question
customer_question = "Can I return a product after 20
days?"

# Generate response
prompt = f"Answer the customer's question based on
the following FAQs:\n{faq_data}\n\nCustomer Question:
{customer_question}"
response = openai.Completion.create(
    model="text-davinci-003",
    prompt=prompt,
    max_tokens=100
)
print(response.choices[0].text.strip())
```
Output:
plaintext

Yes, you can return a product within 30 days of purchase.

Step 4: Analyze Customer Feedback
Task: Use an LLM to identify trends and actionable insights from feedback.
Code Example: Analyzing Feedback
python

```python
# Example feedback dataset
feedback_data = [
```

```
    "Delivery was late, but the product quality is
excellent.",
    "The website is user-friendly, but I wish there
were more payment options.",
    "Customer support took too long to respond to my
query."
]

# Generate insights
prompt = f"Analyze the following customer feedback
and identify trends and improvement
areas:\n{feedback_data}"
response = openai.Completion.create(
    model="text-davinci-003",
    prompt=prompt,
    max_tokens=150
)
print(response.choices[0].text.strip())
```

Output:
plaintext

Trends:
1. Customers appreciate product quality and website usability.
2. Common issues include delayed deliveries, limited payment options,
and slow customer support.

Recommendations:
1. Improve delivery timelines by optimizing logistics.
2. Expand payment options to include additional methods.
3. Enhance customer support response times by adding more agents or
automating common queries.

Step 5: Build a Simple Interactive Application
**Task: Combine FAQ automation and feedback analysis into a single
application.**
Code Example: Interactive Application
python

```
import streamlit as st
```

```python
# FAQ automation
def get_faq_response(question):
    faq_data = {
        "What is your return policy?": "You can
return items within 30 days of purchase.",
        "How do I track my order?": "Use the tracking
link sent to your email.",
        "What payment methods do you accept?": "We
accept credit cards, PayPal, and Apple Pay."
    }
    prompt = f"Answer the customer's question based
on the following FAQs:\n{faq_data}\n\nCustomer
Question: {question}"
    response = openai.Completion.create(
        model="text-davinci-003",
        prompt=prompt,
        max_tokens=100
    )
    return response.choices[0].text.strip()

# Feedback analysis
def analyze_feedback(feedback):
    prompt = f"Analyze the following customer
feedback and identify trends and improvement
areas:\n{feedback}"
    response = openai.Completion.create(
        model="text-davinci-003",
        prompt=prompt,
        max_tokens=150
    )
    return response.choices[0].text.strip()

# Streamlit app
st.title("LLM-Powered Customer Support")

# FAQ automation section
st.header("FAQ Automation")
customer_question = st.text_input("Ask a question:")
```

```
if customer_question:
    faq_response =
get_faq_response(customer_question)
    st.write("Response:", faq_response)

# Feedback analysis section
st.header("Feedback Analysis")
feedback_data = st.text_area("Enter customer feedback
(one per line):")
if feedback_data:
    feedback_list = feedback_data.split("\n")
    insights = analyze_feedback(feedback_list)
    st.write("Insights:", insights)
Run the app using:
bash
```

```bash
streamlit run app.py
```

Step 6: Evaluate the Results
Metrics for Success
1. **FAQ Response Accuracy**:
   - Measure how often the automated responses match customer expectations.
2. **Feedback Insights**:
   - Assess the relevance and actionability of insights generated by the LLM.
3. **Customer Satisfaction**:
   - Use surveys to measure improvements in satisfaction rates after implementing LLM solutions.

Benefits of LLM-Powered Solutions

Aspect	Benefit
Efficiency	Reduces response times for FAQs, freeing up support staff.
Scalability	Handles large volumes of queries and feedback effortlessly.
Actionable	Provides clear recommendations for improving

Aspect	Benefit
Insights	customer experience.

This interactive project demonstrates the practical application of LLMs in solving a business problem. By automating FAQ responses and analyzing customer feedback, companies can enhance operational efficiency and improve customer satisfaction. With its scalability and adaptability, this solution can be customized for businesses across various industries, making LLMs an indispensable tool in the modern business landscape.

7.6 Key Takeaways

7.6.1 Lessons from Real-World Applications

Large Language Models (LLMs) have demonstrated transformative potential across a range of industries, including retail, healthcare, finance, education, manufacturing, and beyond. This section consolidates the lessons learned from real-world applications explored in this chapter, providing actionable insights for businesses and professionals seeking to leverage LLMs.

1. Versatility Across Industries

LLMs are not limited to a single domain but offer solutions tailored to diverse industries. Their flexibility lies in their ability to:

- Process structured and unstructured data.
- Provide actionable insights in natural language.
- Automate complex workflows across sectors.

Examples of Versatility

Industry	Application	Outcome
Retail	Product recommendations	Increased customer satisfaction and sales.
Healthcare	Summarizing patient records	Faster diagnostics and improved accuracy.
Finance	Fraud detection and portfolio optimization	Enhanced security and better investment decisions.
Education	Personalizing learning pathways	Higher student engagement and outcomes.

Industry	Application	Outcome
Manufacturing	Automating quality analysis	Reduced defects and operational efficiency.

2. Lessons from Real-World Applications

2.1 Leverage Data as a Strategic Asset

- **Lesson**: High-quality, well-structured data is essential for effective LLM applications.
- **Example**: In finance, fraud detection relies on comprehensive transaction data to identify anomalies accurately.

Actionable Tip: Invest in data cleaning and integration processes to ensure that inputs for LLMs are reliable and representative.

2.2 Automate Repetitive Tasks

- **Lesson**: LLMs excel at automating repetitive tasks, freeing up human resources for higher-value work.
- **Example**: Automating FAQ responses in customer support reduces response times and improves efficiency.

Actionable Tip: Start by automating simple, high-volume tasks, then expand to more complex workflows as confidence grows.

2.3 Enhance Decision-Making

- **Lesson**: LLMs provide actionable insights by synthesizing vast amounts of data, improving the quality of decisions.
- **Example**: Portfolio optimization in finance leverages LLMs to balance risk and return effectively.

Actionable Tip: Use LLMs to simulate scenarios and evaluate outcomes before making critical business decisions.

2.4 Foster Personalization

- **Lesson**: Personalized recommendations and feedback enhance user engagement and satisfaction.
- **Example**: In education, personalized learning pathways tailored to student needs improve learning outcomes.

Actionable Tip: Implement feedback loops to refine LLM recommendations based on user behavior and preferences.

2.5 Address Industry-Specific Challenges

- **Lesson**: Tailoring LLMs to the specific challenges of an industry increases their effectiveness.
- **Example**: In manufacturing, LLMs integrated with computer vision streamline defect detection and reporting.

Actionable Tip: Customize prompts, datasets, and workflows to align with industry-specific requirements.

2.6 Prioritize Ethical and Responsible Use
- **Lesson**: Transparency, fairness, and privacy are critical considerations when deploying LLMs.
- **Example**: In healthcare, summarizing patient records requires strict adherence to data privacy regulations like HIPAA.

Actionable Tip: Establish ethical guidelines for LLM usage and train teams on responsible AI practices.

3. Benefits of LLM Integration

Aspect	Benefit
Scalability	Handles large volumes of data and requests efficiently.
Accuracy	Reduces errors in repetitive tasks and decision-making processes.
Cost-Effectiveness	Optimizes resource allocation, reducing operational costs.
User Experience	Enhances engagement through personalized interactions and recommendations.

4. Challenges and Solutions

Challenge	Solution
Data Quality Issues	Implement robust data cleaning and validation processes.
Bias in LLM Outputs	Train LLMs on diverse datasets and regularly audit outputs for fairness.
Lack of Industry Expertise	Collaborate with domain experts to fine-tune prompts and interpret insights.

Challenge	Solution
Integration Complexities	Use modular frameworks and APIs for seamless integration into workflows.

5. Looking Ahead

As LLM technology continues to evolve, the following trends are likely to shape its future applications:

1. **Increased Accessibility**:
   - Affordable and user-friendly tools will make LLMs accessible to small and medium-sized enterprises.
2. **Real-Time Applications**:
   - Integration with IoT and edge computing will enable real-time decision-making.
3. **Enhanced Interoperability**:
   - Cross-platform compatibility will streamline adoption across different industries and ecosystems.

The lessons from real-world applications of LLMs emphasize their transformative potential across industries. By leveraging data effectively, automating workflows, and personalizing experiences, organizations can achieve significant efficiency gains, cost savings, and user satisfaction. As businesses continue to integrate LLMs into their operations, they unlock opportunities for innovation, growth, and long-term success.

Chapter 8: Advanced Topics and Future Trends

Large Language Models (LLMs) are immensely powerful out of the box, but fine-tuning these models can significantly enhance their performance for specific use cases. This chapter focuses on fine-tuning LLMs for data workflows, discussing when and why fine-tuning is necessary, along with the tools and techniques that make it possible.

8.1 Fine-Tuning LLMs for Data Workflows

Fine-tuning involves adapting a pre-trained LLM to perform better on a specialized task or dataset. By training the model on additional domain-specific data, organizations can achieve higher accuracy, relevance, and usability for their specific workflows.

8.1.1 When and Why to Fine-Tune

Fine-tuning may not always be required, but certain scenarios make it essential. Understanding when and why to fine-tune is crucial to determining if this step will provide significant value.

1. When to Fine-Tune

1.1 Domain-Specific Requirements

- **Example**: A healthcare company might need an LLM fine-tuned on medical terminology and patient record structures to generate accurate diagnostic summaries.

1.2 Task-Specific Performance

- **Example**: An e-commerce business could fine-tune an LLM to improve the accuracy of product recommendations based on customer preferences.

1.3 Reducing Errors

- Fine-tuning is essential when pre-trained models struggle with domain-specific jargon or uncommon use cases.

Scenario	Pre-Trained Model Limitations	Solution

Scenario	Pre-Trained Model Limitations	Solution
Customer Support Automation	Generic responses unsuitable for niche industries	Fine-tune on industry-specific FAQs
Financial Risk Analysis	Difficulty interpreting financial reports	Train on financial datasets
Healthcare Diagnostics	Limited understanding of medical terms	Fine-tune with medical texts

2. Why Fine-Tune

2.1 Improved Accuracy

Fine-tuning aligns the model's outputs more closely with the requirements of the task or domain.

Example: A fine-tuned model trained on customer service scripts provides more relevant responses than a generic model.

2.2 Tailored Vocabulary

Fine-tuning helps the model understand specific terminologies or jargon.

Example: A legal firm fine-tunes an LLM to interpret legal briefs and contracts accurately.

2.3 Enhanced Efficiency

Fine-tuning reduces the need for extensive prompt engineering, as the model is already optimized for specific workflows.

Example: Instead of crafting detailed prompts, a fine-tuned retail chatbot can provide accurate product recommendations with minimal input.

3. When Not to Fine-Tune

1. **General Use Cases**:
   - If the task involves basic language understanding or generic use, pre-trained models may suffice.
2. **Cost and Resource Constraints**:
   - Fine-tuning requires computational resources and expertise, which might be impractical for smaller organizations.

8.1.2 Tools and Techniques for Fine-Tuning

Fine-tuning requires selecting the right tools and techniques based on the model, dataset, and desired outcome. This section explores the most popular methods and platforms for fine-tuning LLMs.

1. Tools for Fine-Tuning
1.1 Hugging Face Transformers
- Hugging Face offers a robust library for fine-tuning LLMs such as GPT, BERT, and T5.
- Includes pre-built models, datasets, and utilities for training.

Code Example: Fine-Tuning a GPT Model

python

```python
from transformers import GPT2Tokenizer,
GPT2LMHeadModel, Trainer, TrainingArguments

# Load pre-trained model and tokenizer
model = GPT2LMHeadModel.from_pretrained("gpt2")
tokenizer = GPT2Tokenizer.from_pretrained("gpt2")

# Load dataset (example with Hugging Face's datasets
library)
from datasets import load_dataset
dataset = load_dataset("imdb")   # Fine-tuning on
movie reviews

# Tokenize dataset
def tokenize_function(examples):
    return tokenizer(examples["text"],
truncation=True, padding="max_length",
max_length=512)

tokenized_dataset = dataset.map(tokenize_function,
batched=True)

# Training arguments
training_args = TrainingArguments(
    output_dir="./results",
    evaluation_strategy="epoch",
    learning_rate=5e-5,
```

```
    per_device_train_batch_size=8,
    num_train_epochs=3,
)

# Fine-tuning with Trainer API
trainer = Trainer(
    model=model,
    args=training_args,
    train_dataset=tokenized_dataset["train"],
    eval_dataset=tokenized_dataset["test"],
)
trainer.train()
```

1.2 OpenAI Fine-Tuning API
- Allows fine-tuning of OpenAI models like GPT-3 on custom datasets.
- Straightforward process for businesses using OpenAI APIs.

Steps for Fine-Tuning GPT-3:
1. Prepare a JSONL file containing training examples.
2. Use OpenAI CLI to upload the dataset and start fine-tuning.

Command Example:
bash

```
openai api fine_tunes.create -t "data.jsonl" -m
"davinci"
```

1.3 Google Vertex AI
- Offers tools for fine-tuning LLMs on Google Cloud.
- Scales easily for enterprise applications.

1.4 AutoNLP by Hugging Face
- A no-code/low-code platform for fine-tuning models.
- Ideal for organizations without extensive ML expertise.

2. Techniques for Fine-Tuning
2.1 Supervised Fine-Tuning
- Uses labeled datasets to train the model for specific tasks.
- Example: Training a model to classify customer feedback into positive, neutral, or negative sentiments.

2.2 Transfer Learning

- Leverages the knowledge of a pre-trained model and adapts it to a new task or domain.
- Example: Adapting GPT-3 trained on general text to work in the legal domain.

2.3 Reinforcement Learning with Human Feedback (RLHF)

- Combines human evaluations with reinforcement learning to fine-tune LLMs.
- Commonly used in chatbots and recommendation systems.

2.4 Few-Shot Fine-Tuning

- Uses a small dataset to adapt the model to a specific task.
- Example: Fine-tuning an LLM for generating product descriptions with a few hundred examples.

3. Best Practices

Aspect	Best Practice
Data Quality	Use clean, diverse, and representative datasets.
Resource Management	Choose efficient training configurations to minimize costs.
Model Evaluation	Regularly validate the model's performance on test data.
Ethical Considerations	Ensure datasets are unbiased and adhere to privacy laws.

4. Common Challenges and Solutions

Challenge	Solution
Overfitting	Use early stopping and cross-validation during training.
Dataset Bias	Curate diverse datasets to reduce bias in outputs.
High Computational Costs	Use cloud-based platforms or low-precision training methods.

Fine-tuning LLMs offers immense potential to improve task-specific performance, align outputs with business needs, and unlock the full potential of AI in data workflows. By understanding when and why to fine-tune and leveraging the right tools and techniques, businesses can achieve superior results tailored to their specific challenges. Fine-tuning bridges the gap between generic AI models and industry-specific applications, making it an essential strategy in advanced AI deployments.

8.2 Building Custom LLM Applications

Building custom LLM applications allows businesses to tailor AI solutions for specific workflows, enhancing their operational efficiency and effectiveness. This section focuses on two critical aspects of building custom LLM applications: creating pipelines using LangChain and Hugging Face, and deploying LLM-powered APIs in production environments.

8.2.1 Creating Pipelines with LangChain and Hugging Face
1. Overview
Pipelines simplify the process of integrating LLMs into applications by orchestrating tasks such as data preprocessing, model inference, and post-processing. Tools like **LangChain** and **Hugging Face Transformers** offer powerful frameworks for building pipelines tailored to custom use cases.

2. LangChain Pipelines
LangChain is designed to create pipelines that connect LLMs with external tools, data sources, and workflows. It enables complex applications such as chatbots, document retrieval, and decision-making systems.

Example: Building a Customer Support Pipeline
Use Case:
- Automate responses to customer queries using an LLM and integrate with a database for FAQ retrieval.

Code Example:

python

```python
from langchain.chains import RetrievalQA
from langchain.vectorstores import FAISS
from langchain.document_loaders import TextLoader
from langchain.llms import OpenAI

# Load FAQs into a vector store
loader = TextLoader("faqs.txt")  # File containing
FAQ data
documents = loader.load()
vector_store = FAISS.from_documents(documents)

# Initialize LLM and Retrieval Chain
llm = OpenAI(model="text-davinci-003", temperature=0)
qa_chain = RetrievalQA(llm=llm,
retriever=vector_store.as_retriever())

# Ask a question
query = "How do I return an item?"
response = qa_chain.run(query)
print("Response:", response)
```

Key Features of LangChain
- **Document Retrieval**: Integrates with vector databases for semantic search.
- **Tool Integration**: Combines LLMs with tools like calculators, databases, and APIs.
- **Agent Frameworks**: Allows dynamic decision-making by chaining multiple tools.

3. Hugging Face Pipelines
Hugging Face provides pre-built pipelines for various NLP tasks, such as text classification, summarization, and translation. These pipelines can be easily customized for specific applications.

Example: Summarization Pipeline
Use Case:
- Summarize lengthy customer feedback for analysis.

Code Example:
python

```python
from transformers import pipeline

# Load summarization pipeline
summarizer = pipeline("summarization",
model="facebook/bart-large-cnn")

# Summarize feedback
feedback = """
I recently purchased your product, and while the
quality was excellent, the delivery was delayed by a
week. The customer service team was helpful, but the
overall experience could be improved.
"""
summary = summarizer(feedback, max_length=50,
min_length=25, do_sample=False)
print("Summary:", summary[0]["summary_text"])
```

Output:
sql

```
The product quality was excellent, but the delivery was delayed.
Customer service was helpful, but improvements are needed overall.
```

Key Features of Hugging Face Pipelines
- **Ease of Use**: Pre-configured pipelines for common tasks.
- **Extensibility**: Customize pipelines with fine-tuned models.
- **Wide Model Support**: Access to a vast library of pre-trained models.

---

4. Building a Combined Pipeline
Integrate LangChain and Hugging Face for more complex workflows, such as customer sentiment analysis followed by personalized recommendations.
Code Example:

python

```python
from langchain.chains import SequentialChain
from transformers import pipeline

# Sentiment analysis with Hugging Face
sentiment_analyzer = pipeline("sentiment-analysis")

def analyze_sentiment(text):
    result = sentiment_analyzer(text)
    return result[0]["label"]

# Recommendation system with LangChain
from langchain.chains import LLMChain
from langchain.prompts import PromptTemplate

recommendation_prompt = PromptTemplate(
    input_variables=["sentiment"],
    template="Based on a {sentiment} sentiment,
recommend a product."
)
recommendation_chain =
LLMChain(llm=OpenAI(model="text-davinci-003"),
prompt=recommendation_prompt)

# Combine into a sequential pipeline
pipeline = SequentialChain(chains=[analyze_sentiment,
recommendation_chain])
response = pipeline.run("I love the product, but I
found the price a bit high.")
print("Response:", response)
```

8.2.2 Deploying LLM-Powered APIs in Production
1. Overview
Deploying LLM-powered APIs allows businesses to integrate AI capabilities into their production environments, enabling seamless user interactions and automated processes. This involves creating endpoints

for real-time model inference, ensuring scalability, security, and maintainability.

2. Steps for API Deployment
Step 1: API Development
Use frameworks like **FastAPI** or **Flask** to expose the LLM as a RESTful API.
Code Example: FastAPI LLM Endpoint
python

```python
from fastapi import FastAPI
from transformers import pipeline

# Initialize FastAPI app and pipeline
app = FastAPI()
qa_pipeline = pipeline("question-answering",
model="distilbert-base-uncased")

@app.post("/qa")
def answer_question(question: str, context: str):
    result = qa_pipeline(question=question,
context=context)
    return {"answer": result["answer"]}

# Run the server
# Use `uvicorn main:app --reload` to start the
FastAPI server.
```

Step 2: Containerization
Use Docker to containerize the API for portability and easy deployment.
Dockerfile Example:
dockerfile

```dockerfile
FROM python:3.9-slim
WORKDIR /app
COPY requirements.txt .
RUN pip install -r requirements.txt
COPY . .
CMD ["uvicorn", "main:app", "--host", "0.0.0.0", "--port", "8000"]
```

Step 3: Cloud Deployment

Deploy the API using platforms like AWS, Google Cloud, or Azure for scalability.

Example: Deploying on AWS Lambda

1. Package the app using serverless framework.
2. Upload the container to AWS Elastic Container Registry (ECR).
3. Configure API Gateway to route requests to the Lambda function.

3. Best Practices for Production Deployment

Aspect	Best Practice
Scalability	Use load balancers and autoscaling to handle traffic spikes.
Security	Implement authentication (e.g., API keys, OAuth).
Monitoring	Integrate logging and monitoring tools to track API usage.
Cost Optimization	Use serverless architectures or GPU-based instances wisely.

4. Example Use Case: LLM-Powered Recommendation API

Scenario:

An e-commerce company needs a real-time recommendation API for their website.

Pipeline:

1. Analyze user behavior with Hugging Face.
2. Generate personalized recommendations with LangChain.
3. Serve recommendations via a FastAPI endpoint.

Building custom LLM applications with LangChain and Hugging Face and deploying them via APIs enables organizations to integrate AI capabilities seamlessly into their workflows. By leveraging these tools and following best practices, businesses can create scalable, secure, and efficient solutions tailored to their unique challenges and goals.

8.3 Multimodal Capabilities

Multimodal LLMs represent a significant leap forward in artificial intelligence, enabling models to process and integrate information from multiple data formats, such as text, tabular data, and visual inputs. This chapter explores the integration of diverse data types into workflows and examines emerging trends shaping the future of multimodal LLMs.

8.3.1 Combining Text, Tabular Data, and Visual Inputs

1. Overview

Multimodal LLMs process and interpret multiple data types, combining them into unified outputs. This ability is crucial for applications where decisions rely on diverse data sources, such as medical diagnostics (text and imaging) or business intelligence (text and tabular data).

2. Applications of Multimodal Capabilities

2.1 Healthcare

- Combine patient notes (text), lab results (tabular), and X-rays (images) for diagnosis.

2.2 Business Analytics

- Integrate sales reports (tabular), customer feedback (text), and marketing visuals to generate actionable insights.

2.3 Retail

- Use product descriptions (text), pricing data (tabular), and product images (visual) for dynamic recommendations.

3. Example Workflow: Multimodal Data Integration

Scenario

A retail company analyzes product reviews (text), sales data (tabular), and product images (visual) to identify top-performing products.

Step 1: Data Preparation

Input Data

- **Textual**: Customer reviews.
- **Tabular**: Sales performance metrics.
- **Visual**: Product images.

Example Dataset

Product	Reviews (Text)	Sales ($)	Image (File)
Product A	"Excellent quality, highly recommend."	20,000	product_a.jpg
Product B	"Average quality, overpriced."	10,000	product_b.jpg

Step 2: Model Integration
Code Example: Multimodal Data Analysis
python

```python
from transformers import pipeline
import pandas as pd
from PIL import Image

# Load pipelines
text_analyzer = pipeline("sentiment-analysis")
image_classifier = pipeline("image-classification",
model="google/vit-base-patch16-224")

# Tabular data
data = pd.DataFrame({
    "Product": ["Product A", "Product B"],
    "Reviews": ["Excellent quality, highly
recommend.", "Average quality, overpriced."],
    "Sales": [20000, 10000],
    "Image": ["product_a.jpg", "product_b.jpg"]
})

# Analyze text and images
for index, row in data.iterrows():
    text_sentiment = text_analyzer(row["Reviews"])[0]
    image_analysis =
image_classifier(Image.open(row["Image"]))
    print(f"Product: {row['Product']}")
    print(f"Sentiment: {text_sentiment['label']} with
score {text_sentiment['score']}")
    print(f"Top Image Classification:
{image_analysis[0]['label']} with score
{image_analysis[0]['score']}")
    print(f"Sales: ${row['Sales']}")
```

Step 3: Unified Output
Generated Insights:
- Product A is highly rated and has strong sales; recommend
  expanding inventory.

- Product B shows poor sentiment and lower sales; consider revising pricing or promotions.

4. Benefits of Multimodal Data Integration

Aspect	Benefit
Comprehensive Insights	Combines multiple data perspectives for richer analysis.
Enhanced Accuracy	Reduces biases inherent in single-modality models.
Actionable Results	Generates holistic recommendations for complex decisions.

8.3.2 Emerging Trends in Multimodal LLMs
1. Overview
The field of multimodal LLMs is rapidly evolving, with advancements enabling models to process increasingly diverse inputs. Emerging trends highlight the future direction of these technologies.

2. Key Trends
2.1 Unified Multimodal Models
- Models like OpenAI's GPT-4 and Google's PaLM-E are designed to handle text, image, and tabular inputs within a single architecture.

Example: A single query to GPT-4 that includes a product image, sales data, and a customer query can return insights combining all these modalities.

2.2 Real-Time Multimodal Processing
- Future models aim to analyze multimodal data streams in real time.
- **Use Case**: A self-driving car processes visual (camera feeds), textual (maps), and tabular (sensor readings) data simultaneously.

2.3 Enhanced Visual Understanding

- Vision Transformer (ViT)-based models are improving in their ability to interpret complex visual inputs, such as medical imaging or architectural blueprints.

Example: Diagnosing diseases by integrating patient history (text) with MRI scans (visual).

2.4 Natural Interaction with Multimodal Inputs
- Models are being trained to interpret human instructions combining modalities.
- **Example**: A user uploads a spreadsheet and an image, asking, "How do these numbers correlate with the image trends?"

3. Challenges in Multimodal Integration

Challenge	Description	Solution
Data Alignment	Ensuring text, images, and tables are correctly matched.	Use multimodal datasets with precise annotations.
Computational Costs	Processing multimodal inputs requires significant resources.	Optimize models with parameter-efficient training techniques.
Interpreting Outputs	Combining insights from multiple modalities can be complex.	Develop frameworks to aggregate and contextualize results.

4. Future Applications

Domain	Application
Healthcare	Combining clinical notes, lab results, and medical images for diagnostics.
Finance	Integrating financial reports, stock charts, and news articles for investment analysis.
Retail	Analyzing customer reviews, sales data, and product images for inventory optimization.

Multimodal capabilities in LLMs unlock new possibilities for handling complex, real-world tasks by integrating diverse data formats into a unified analysis. The ability to combine text, tabular data, and visuals paves the way for more accurate and actionable insights across industries. As emerging trends enhance these models, their applications will expand, driving innovation and efficiency in areas such as healthcare, finance, and beyond.

8.4 Community Engagement

Engaging with the AI and data science community offers numerous benefits, including access to cutting-edge knowledge, opportunities for collaboration, and the chance to contribute to open-source projects. This section explores the importance of joining AI/data science communities and contributing to open-source initiatives, providing actionable steps to enhance your involvement in these activities.

8.4.1 Joining AI/Data Science Communities

1. Overview

AI and data science communities are hubs of knowledge exchange, networking, and professional development. By becoming an active participant, you can stay updated on the latest trends, learn from experts, and collaborate with peers.

2. Benefits of Joining Communities

Benefit	Description
Knowledge Sharing	Gain insights into emerging technologies, best practices, and innovative ideas.
Networking Opportunities	Build connections with industry experts, researchers, and like-minded peers.
Collaboration	Participate in collaborative projects, competitions, and research initiatives.
Career Growth	Access job opportunities, mentorship, and skill development resources.

3. Popular AI/Data Science Communities

Community	Platform	Focus
Kaggle	Kaggle.com	Data science competitions and learning.
Hugging Face Forums	HuggingFace.co	NLP and machine learning discussions.

Community	Platform	Focus
AI Alignment Forum	AlignmentForum.org	Ethical AI and advanced AI research.
Reddit	r/MachineLearning, etc.	Broad discussions on AI and data science.
LinkedIn Groups	LinkedIn	Professional networking and resources.

4. Steps to Join and Engage

Step 1: Choose the Right Community

- Select communities that align with your interests and expertise.

Step 2: Participate Actively

- Engage in discussions, ask questions, and share your knowledge.

Step 3: Attend Events

- Join webinars, hackathons, and meetups to connect with others.

Step 4: Leverage Resources

- Use tutorials, datasets, and tools shared by the community to enhance your skills.

5. Example: Joining Kaggle

Kaggle is a popular platform for data scientists and AI enthusiasts.

Steps to Get Started

1. Create an account at Kaggle.com.
2. Explore competitions, datasets, and discussion forums.
3. Participate in your first competition by downloading the dataset and submitting a model.

Code Example: Using a Kaggle Dataset

python

```
import pandas as pd

# Load a dataset from Kaggle
# Example: Titanic dataset
data = pd.read_csv("titanic.csv")
print(data.head())
```

8.4.2 Contributing to Open-Source Projects

1. Overview
Open-source contributions drive innovation and provide an excellent opportunity to collaborate with the global AI and data science community. By contributing to open-source projects, you can enhance your skills, build your portfolio, and give back to the community.

2. Benefits of Open-Source Contributions

Benefit	Description
Skill Development	Gain hands-on experience in coding, documentation, and project management.
Community Recognition	Establish your reputation within the AI and data science community.
Learning Opportunities	Learn best practices and new techniques from experienced contributors.
Portfolio Building	Showcase your work to potential employers or collaborators.

3. Finding Open-Source Projects

Platform	Focus
GitHub	Repositories on every imaginable AI topic.
Hugging Face Hub	NLP and machine learning projects.
TensorFlow Projects	AI tools and frameworks.
PyTorch Projects	PyTorch-based AI models and utilities.

Popular Projects to Contribute
- **Transformers** (Hugging Face): NLP models and pipelines.
- **TensorFlow**: Open-source machine learning platform.
- **PyTorch Lightning**: Simplifies AI model training.
- **Scikit-learn**: Machine learning library in Python.

4. Steps to Contribute
Step 1: Identify a Project
- Explore repositories on platforms like GitHub or Hugging Face that match your interests.

Step 2: Understand the Project
- Read the README file and explore the documentation to understand the project's purpose.

Step 3: Choose a Contribution

- Contribute to code, documentation, testing, or issue resolution.

Step 4: Fork and Clone the Repository

bash

```
# Clone a repository
git clone
https://github.com/<username>/<repository>.git
```

Step 5: Create a Branch and Make Changes

bash

```
# Create a new branch
git checkout -b feature-addition

# Commit changes
git add .
git commit -m "Added a new feature"
```

Step 6: Submit a Pull Request

- Push your changes to the forked repository and submit a pull request to the original project.

---

5. Example: Contributing to Hugging Face Transformers

Objective: Add a new example script for fine-tuning a model.

Steps:

1. Fork the Transformers repository.
2. Create a script for fine-tuning a model on a specific dataset.
3. Test the script and ensure it aligns with project standards.
4. Submit a pull request with your changes.

Code Example:

python

```
from transformers import BertTokenizer,
BertForSequenceClassification, Trainer,
TrainingArguments

# Load model and tokenizer
tokenizer = BertTokenizer.from_pretrained("bert-base-
uncased")
```

```
model =
BertForSequenceClassification.from_pretrained("bert-
base-uncased")

# Tokenize data
train_data = ["This is a positive example.", "This is
a negative example."]
labels = [1, 0]
inputs = tokenizer(train_data, padding=True,
truncation=True, return_tensors="pt")
inputs["labels"] = torch.tensor(labels)

# Training arguments
training_args =
TrainingArguments(output_dir="./results",
num_train_epochs=3, per_device_train_batch_size=8)

# Trainer
trainer = Trainer(model=model, args=training_args,
train_dataset=inputs)
trainer.train()
```

6. Overcoming Challenges in Open-Source Contributions

Challenge	Solution
Understanding the Codebase	Start with small contributions, such as fixing typos in documentation.
Technical Knowledge Gap	Learn from the project's documentation and ask questions in the community.
Rejection of Contributions	Accept feedback positively and use it to improve future contributions.

Engaging with AI and data science communities and contributing to open-source projects is an invaluable way to grow as a professional. These activities foster collaboration, skill development, and networking, while also allowing you to give back to the broader community. Whether joining forums, participating in competitions, or enhancing open-source repositories, these efforts build a stronger foundation for your career in AI and data science.

8.5 Future-Proofing Your Skills

The rapid evolution of artificial intelligence (AI) and data science necessitates continuous learning and adaptation to remain competitive. Staying ahead of technological advancements is essential for professionals who want to future-proof their skills and maintain relevance in a fast-changing landscape. This section provides practical strategies and tools to ensure you stay ahead in the field.

8.5.1 Staying Ahead of Technological Advancements
1. The Importance of Staying Updated
Technological advancements in AI, machine learning, and data science frequently introduce new tools, methodologies, and paradigms. Staying current offers several benefits:
- **Enhanced Employability**: Keeping up with trends makes you a valuable asset to organizations.
- **Career Growth**: Early adoption of emerging technologies positions you as an industry leader.
- **Problem-Solving**: Modern tools and methods improve your efficiency in tackling complex challenges.

2. Strategies to Stay Ahead
2.1 Continuous Learning
Commit to lifelong learning to keep pace with advancements.
Resources for Learning:

Platform	Focus	Example
Coursera	Courses from universities and companies	Machine Learning by Stanford University
edX	Professional certificates	MIT's AI for Everyone
Udemy	Practical and affordable courses	Python for Data Science and Machine Learning
YouTube Channels	Tutorials and tech updates	AI Coffee Break, 3Blue1Brown

Practical Example: Enrolling in a New Course
python

```
# Suggestion: Join Andrew Ng's Deep Learning
Specialization on Coursera
print("Learn about advanced neural networks and
modern AI techniques.")
```

2.2 Master Emerging Tools

Learning and adopting the latest tools ensures you can leverage cutting-edge capabilities in your workflows.

Category	Tool Examples
Machine Learning	TensorFlow, PyTorch
Data Analysis	pandas, Apache Spark
Visualization	Plotly, Tableau
NLP Models	Hugging Face Transformers, LangChain

Code Example: Exploring Hugging Face Transformers

python

```
from transformers import pipeline

# Sentiment analysis using Hugging Face Transformers
analyzer = pipeline("sentiment-analysis")
result = analyzer("The advancements in AI are
incredible!")
print(result)
```

Output:

css

```
[{'label': 'POSITIVE', 'score': 0.9998}]
```

2.3 Engage in Hands-On Projects

Apply your knowledge by building real-world projects. These projects showcase your expertise and keep your skills sharp.

Examples of Projects:

1. Develop a recommendation system for an e-commerce platform.
2. Build a chatbot using LLMs for customer support.
3. Analyze stock market trends using time-series models.

2.4 Follow Industry Trends

Stay informed about industry news, research papers, and advancements through:
- **News Platforms**: *AI Trends, Towards Data Science, MIT Technology Review.*
- **Research Platforms**: *arXiv, Papers with Code.*
- **Social Media**: Follow AI researchers and companies on LinkedIn and Twitter.

2.5 Attend Conferences and Webinars
Conferences and webinars provide exposure to the latest innovations and networking opportunities.

Event	Focus
NeurIPS	Machine learning research and applications
ICLR	Representation learning techniques
AI Expo	Industry use cases and applications

3. Staying Ahead in Specific AI Domains
3.1 Natural Language Processing (NLP)
- **Current Focus**: LLMs like GPT-4, fine-tuning, and prompt engineering.
- **Future Direction**: Multimodal models and real-time NLP.

Actionable Step: Explore tools like LangChain for building conversational agents.

3.2 Computer Vision
- **Current Focus**: Vision Transformers (ViT) and object detection.
- **Future Direction**: 3D modeling, augmented reality, and medical imaging.

Actionable Step: Experiment with Vision Transformer models using Hugging Face.

3.3 Data Engineering
- **Current Focus**: Data pipelines, big data platforms.
- **Future Direction**: Real-time streaming and cloud-native solutions.

Actionable Step: Learn Apache Kafka for handling real-time data.

4. Build a Personal Brand

Create a professional presence to showcase your expertise.

4.1 Publish Content

- Write blogs on platforms like Medium or LinkedIn.
- Publish tutorials and guides.

4.2 Contribute to Open Source

- Join repositories on GitHub.
- Collaborate on popular projects in AI and data science.

Code Example: Sharing a Repository

bash

```
# Create a new GitHub repository for a personal
project
git init
git add .
git commit -m "Initial commit"
git remote add origin
https://github.com/yourusername/yourproject.git
git push -u origin main
```

4.3 Present at Conferences

- Share your projects and research findings with a broader audience.

5. Adopt a Growth Mindset

Staying ahead of technological advancements requires a mindset geared toward continuous improvement.

Best Practices:

- **Embrace Change**: View new technologies as opportunities.
- **Learn from Failures**: Treat setbacks as learning experiences.
- **Seek Feedback**: Regularly request constructive feedback from peers and mentors.

6. Challenges and Solutions

Challenge	Solution
Overwhelming Amount of Information	Focus on one skill or technology at a time to avoid burnout.
Rapid Technological Changes	Join communities to learn about updates and best practices quickly.

Challenge	Solution
Lack of Practical Experience	Engage in hands-on projects and open-source contributions.

Future-proofing your skills in AI and data science requires a proactive approach to learning, adapting, and engaging with the community. By mastering emerging tools, building hands-on projects, following industry trends, and maintaining a growth mindset, you can ensure that you stay at the forefront of technological advancements, ready to tackle the challenges and opportunities of tomorrow.

8.6 Key Takeaways

8.6.1 Skills for the Future of LLM-Driven Data Workflows
As Large Language Models (LLMs) continue to revolutionize data workflows, professionals must adapt to new tools, techniques, and paradigms to remain competitive. This section summarizes the critical skills needed for leveraging LLMs effectively in the evolving landscape of AI-driven data workflows.

1. Core Technical Skills
1.1 Mastering LLM Ecosystems
Understanding how to work with LLMs, including their training, fine-tuning, and deployment, is essential for designing and managing workflows.
Skills to Develop:
1. **Fine-Tuning Models**:
   - Customize LLMs for domain-specific tasks.
   - Tools: Hugging Face Transformers, OpenAI Fine-Tuning API.
2. **Prompt Engineering**:
   - Craft effective prompts to optimize LLM outputs.
   - Example:

python

```
import openai
response = openai.Completion.create(
```

```
    model="text-davinci-003",
    prompt="Explain how LLMs can improve customer
support workflows.",
    max_tokens=100
)
print(response.choices[0].text.strip())
API Integration:
```
- o Use APIs like OpenAI or Azure OpenAI for embedding LLMs into applications.

1.2 Data Engineering and Processing

LLM-driven workflows often rely on well-prepared data. Proficiency in data engineering ensures that models receive clean, structured, and relevant inputs.

Skills to Develop:

1. **Data Cleaning and Preprocessing**:
   - o Tools: pandas, Apache Spark.
   - o Example:

python

```
import pandas as pd
data = pd.read_csv("data.csv")
clean_data = data.dropna().reset_index(drop=True)
print(clean_data.head())
```

2. **ETL Pipelines**:
   - o Extract, transform, and load data efficiently.
   - o Tools: Apache Kafka, Airflow.
3. **Multimodal Data Handling**:
   - o Integrate text, tabular, and visual data for LLM-driven workflows.

1.3 AI Model Evaluation and Optimization

The ability to evaluate and optimize model performance ensures high-quality outputs and efficiency.

Skills to Develop:

1. **Performance Metrics**:
   - o Use metrics such as BLEU (for text generation), ROUGE (for summarization), or accuracy (for classification).

2. **Error Analysis**:
   - o Identify failure modes in model predictions.
   - o Example: Log and analyze incorrect predictions in customer support automation.
3. **Optimization Techniques**:
   - o Fine-tune hyperparameters and utilize parameter-efficient techniques.

2. Emerging AI-Specific Skills
2.1 Multimodal Data Integration
Future workflows will increasingly rely on integrating multiple data modalities, such as text, images, and tabular data.
Skills to Develop:
1. **Multimodal Model Training**:
   - o Example: Training models to analyze customer reviews (text), sales data (tabular), and product images.
2. **Frameworks and Tools**:
   - o Vision Transformers (ViT), LangChain, Hugging Face.

2.2 Ethical AI Practices
Adopting responsible AI practices ensures fairness, transparency, and compliance in LLM-driven workflows.
Skills to Develop:
1. **Bias Mitigation**:
   - o Identify and address biases in datasets and models.
2. **Privacy and Compliance**:
   - o Ensure adherence to regulations like GDPR or HIPAA when handling sensitive data.

2.3 Collaboration and Cross-Disciplinary Skills
Modern data workflows require collaboration across teams and disciplines.
Skills to Develop:
1. **Cross-Functional Communication**:
   - o Translate technical insights into business value for stakeholders.
2. **Team Collaboration**:

- o Work with data engineers, domain experts, and project managers to develop solutions.

3. Tools and Frameworks Mastery
3.1 LLM-Specific Frameworks

Framework	Key Feature
Hugging Face	Pre-trained models for NLP, multimodal tasks.
LangChain	Building complex LLM applications with workflows.
OpenAI API	Easy integration of GPT-based models into projects.

3.2 Data Engineering Tools

Tool	Key Feature
pandas	Data cleaning and manipulation for structured data.
Apache Spark	Scalable big data processing.
Airflow	Workflow automation for ETL pipelines.

3.3 Deployment Tools

Platform	Key Feature
FastAPI	Building and deploying APIs for LLM applications.
Docker	Containerization for scalable deployments.
AWS Lambda	Serverless LLM deployments for cost efficiency.

4. Soft Skills for the Future
4.1 Adaptability
- Stay open to learning new technologies and adapting to rapid advancements.

4.2 Problem-Solving
- Apply AI solutions creatively to complex, real-world challenges.

4.3 Lifelong Learning
- Regularly update skills through courses, certifications, and community engagement.

5. Preparing for Future Trends
5.1 Continuous Skill Development

- Stay informed about advancements in areas like generative AI, edge computing, and federated learning.

5.2 Focus on Multimodal AI

- Develop expertise in models that combine text, images, and other data types.

To thrive in the era of LLM-driven data workflows, professionals must master a combination of technical, emerging, and soft skills. By staying ahead of technological advancements, building cross-disciplinary expertise, and adopting ethical AI practices, you can ensure your skillset remains future-proof in a rapidly evolving industry.

Appendices

This section serves as a comprehensive guide to supplementary resources, tools, practice datasets, and key terms that enhance your understanding and enable practical learning. Each appendix is crafted to support both beginners and advanced users.

1. Appendix A: Resources

This appendix lists essential books, courses, and websites for deepening your understanding of LLMs, data workflows, and related technologies.

1.1 Recommended Books

Title	Author(s)	Focus
Deep Learning	Ian Goodfellow, Yoshua Bengio, Aaron Courville	Foundational concepts in AI and deep learning.
Hands-On Machine Learning with Scikit-Learn, Keras, and TensorFlow	Aurélien Géron	Practical ML and deep learning with Python.
Natural Language Processing with Transformers	Lewis Tunstall, Leandro von Werra, Thomas Wolf	Hugging Face Transformers for NLP.
Data Science for Business	Foster Provost, Tom Fawcett	Data science principles applied to business scenarios.

1.2 Online Courses

Platform	Course Title	Focus
Coursera	*Machine Learning by Stanford University*	Foundational ML concepts and algorithms.
edX	*AI for Everyone by Andrew Ng*	High-level overview of AI applications.
Udemy	*NLP with Python: Building Chatbots*	Practical NLP for chatbots and beyond.
Kaggle	*Intro to Machine Learning*	Beginner-friendly ML tutorials.

Platform	Course Title	Focus
Learn		

1.3 Recommended Websites

Website	Focus
Hugging Face	Pre-trained models and tools for NLP workflows.
Kaggle	Competitions, datasets, and tutorials.
arXiv	Latest AI research papers.
Towards Data Science	Tutorials and articles on AI and data science.

2. Appendix B: Tools and Frameworks Cheat Sheet

This appendix provides a quick reference to commonly used libraries and APIs for building LLM-driven workflows.

Tool/Library	Purpose	Key Functions
Hugging Face	NLP and multimodal workflows	Pre-trained models, tokenizers, fine-tuning tools.
LangChain	Building LLM-powered applications	Document retrieval, conversational agents.
OpenAI API	GPT-based tasks	Text completion, summarization, coding assistance.
pandas	Data manipulation	DataFrames, cleaning, filtering.
Matplotlib	Data visualization	Line charts, scatter plots, histograms.
PyTorch	Deep learning frameworks	Training custom models, fine-tuning.
FastAPI	API development	Create and deploy RESTful APIs.
Docker	Containerization	Isolate and deploy applications in containers.

Example: Using Hugging Face Transformers

python

```
from transformers import pipeline

# Load a sentiment analysis pipeline
analyzer = pipeline("sentiment-analysis")
result = analyzer("I love learning about LLMs!")
print(result)
```
Output:
css

[{'label': 'POSITIVE', 'score': 0.999}]

---

3. Appendix C: Sample Datasets

Practice datasets for honing skills in querying, visualization, and analysis.

Dataset Name	Description	Source
Titanic Dataset	Passenger data for survival analysis.	Kaggle
Iris Dataset	Classification of iris flower species.	UCI Repository
NYC Taxi Dataset	Data on taxi trips in New York City.	NYC Open Data
IMDB Movie Reviews	Sentiment analysis of movie reviews.	Kaggle

---

Example: Loading a Dataset
python

```
import pandas as pd

# Load Titanic dataset
data = pd.read_csv("titanic.csv")
print(data.head())
```

4. Appendix D: Practice Problems

Test your skills with these problems covering SQL queries, visualization tasks, and analytical challenges.

4.1 SQL Queries

Problem: Write an SQL query to find the top 5 highest-grossing movies from a dataset.

Dataset Structure:

Column	Description
movie_title	Title of the movie.
box_office	Total box office earnings.

Solution:

sql

```sql
SELECT movie_title, box_office
FROM movies
ORDER BY box_office DESC
LIMIT 5;
```

4.2 Visualization Task

Problem: Create a bar chart showing sales by region.

Code Example:

python

```python
import matplotlib.pyplot as plt

# Sales data
regions = ['North', 'South', 'East', 'West']
sales = [50000, 40000, 45000, 30000]

plt.bar(regions, sales)
plt.title("Sales by Region")
plt.xlabel("Region")
plt.ylabel("Sales ($)")
plt.show()
```

4.3 Analysis Scenario

Problem: Identify the top-performing product category based on sales and profitability.

Dataset:

Product	Category	Sales ($)	Profit ($)
Product A	Electronics	50000	10000
Product B	Furniture	30000	5000

Solution:

- Perform aggregation using pandas:

python

```python
import pandas as pd

# Create dataset
data = pd.DataFrame({
    "Category": ["Electronics", "Furniture"],
    "Sales": [50000, 30000],
    "Profit": [10000, 5000]
})

# Calculate profitability
data["Profit Margin (%)"] = (data["Profit"] /
data["Sales"]) * 100
print(data)
```

---

5. Appendix E: Glossary

Term	Definition
LLM	Large Language Model, an AI model trained on extensive text data for various tasks.
Fine-Tuning	Adapting a pre-trained model to a specific dataset or task for improved performance.
Prompt Engineering	Crafting inputs to guide LLMs in generating desired outputs.
Tokenization	The process of breaking text into smaller units, such as words or subwords.
API	Application Programming Interface, allowing

Term	Definition
	interaction with software components.
ETL	Extract, Transform, Load, a process for preparing and managing data pipelines.
Transformer	Neural network architecture underlying most modern LLMs, such as GPT and BERT.
Multimodal	Models capable of processing multiple data types (e.g., text, images, tabular data).

These appendices are designed as a ready reference for tools, concepts, datasets, and problems that support learning and applying LLMs in real-world workflows. Use them as a foundation for building your expertise and advancing your projects.

www.ingramcontent.com/pod-product-compliance
Lightning Source LLC
LaVergne TN
LVHW080113070326
832902LV00015B/2560